C0-AQZ-985

MBO CAN WORK !

MBO CAN WORK!

How to Manage by Contract

Charles R. Macdonald

McGRAW-HILL BOOK COMPANY

New York   St. Louis   San Francisco   Auckland   Bogotá
Hamburg   Johannesburg   London   Madrid   Mexico
Montreal   New Delhi   Panama   Paris   São Paulo
Singapore   Sydney   Tokyo   Toronto

Library of Congress Cataloging in Publication Data

Macdonald, Charles R.
  MBO can work!

  Includes index.
  1. Management by objectives.   I. Title.
HF38.M284   1982   685.4'012   81-4457
ISBN 0-07-044331-9   AACR2

ISBN 0-07-044331-9

1234567890   DODO   8987654321

The editors for this book were William Newton and Iris Cohen,
the designer was Naomi Auerbach, and the production
supervisor was Paul Malchow. It was set in Ballardvale
by World Composition Services.

Printed and bound by R.R. Donnelley & Sons Company.

CONTENTS

PREFACE

PRODUCTIVITY IS THE ISSUE

There are few more crucial and pressing issues facing management today than the need to increase productivity of the business enterprise. Evidence can be found on all sides that we are failing to come to grips with this critical problem. The core of the issue, there is reason to believe, may be in the office, the technical laboratory, and the executive suite, rather than on the production floor—as evidenced by studies which show that the productivity of higher-level employees in the typical organization is considerably below its potential.

What is worse, the low state of productivity in the workplace may be a direct consequence of this white-collar lag, because of unclear work assignments, improper staffing, blocked lines of communication, lack of discipline, and poor example setting.

Unfortunately, no quick and easy solutions are at hand. The problem is deep-seated, complex, and sensitive, and it will not be solved by some new breed of management efficiency expert. It is becoming increasingly clear, nevertheless, that the productivity of management employees *can be* improved materially—and the benefits to the enterprise in the form of increased output and profitability can be quite remarkable.

PURPOSE AND SCOPE OF THIS BOOK

This book is about managerial productivity and how to improve it. It presents and describes a methodology for making management by objectives work in the operating environment. It is written for the general manager of a business organization—whatever title the position carries—and the functional manager who aspires to become a general manager at some time in the future. If you are the first of these, the book can help you make your total organization more productive by increasing the individual and collective productivity of managers, technicians, administrators, and professionals—the "knowledge" workers who form an increasing proportion of our post-industrial economy. If you are the latter, the book can help you make your own function more productive. In the process, you can realize greater personal job satisfaction even while enhancing your value to the organization.

The book is founded on a couple of basic principles of human resource management. One, the ultimate motivator, indeed the ultimate accolade to the individual, is for the organization to demand the very best performance of which the person is capable. To ask less or to accept less is demeaning to the individual. Second, the best goals are the goals that individuals set for themselves within an overall guiding framework of objectives that will energize and motivate people to excel. More often than not, I have found, these goals are the ones that are achieved, even while they tend to be more demanding on the individual.

Management by contract is an attempt to convert these principles into a structured process of management that will help managers of all functional disciplines and on all organization levels to develop more fully their own potential as individuals and as professional managers, while at the same time enhancing the overall productivity of the total enterprise.

MANAGEMENT BY OBJECTIVES AND SELF-CONTROL

During the past 25 years or so, the management discipline called *management by objectives* (MBO) has built a large following in American industry. During this period, MBO has generated a high degree of acceptance for the notion that results are more important than activity and has created a substantial reservoir of goodwill among achieving managers because it gives visibility to competence and promises to reward accomplishment.

This book builds on the foundation of MBO. Management by contract presents an integrated process of managerial productivity improvement using the MBO concept as a central core. It is a system of management by objectives, self-appraisal, and self-control that finds expression in a negotiated "contract" between each manager and his or her organizational superior. The contract documents the understanding reached between them, and represents a formalizing of the commitments of each manager to the other, as well as to the organization. The contract also provides more equitable sharing of responsibility for results, fairer sharing of credit for accomplishment, and more evenhanded sharing of liability for failure.

The management process of which the contract is the centerpiece is a highly developed form of participative management, without being in the least permissive. Neither is it authoritarian. Rather, the process represents a dialogue between people in different functions and on different levels of management based on verifiable facts and conducted in an atmosphere of mutual respect and regard for individual worth.

I have taken the position—as others have before me—that management by objectives and self-control must be built into the management structure, not tacked on as a separate subsystem. Truly effective MBO should permeate every function, should govern every activity, and should be integrated into every planning and control subsystem. In this way, the MBO process becomes the process of management itself. Management by contract has been designed to meet these essential criteria. The process does so, moreover, in a nondestructive fashion—without tearing down the existing management structure in order to erect a new one in its place.

RECONCILING GOALS

Management by contract proposes a solution to a particularly troublesome problem of MBO—that of reconciling individual managers' objectives with those of other people and with the larger goals of the total organization. This is accomplished by means of a unique process within a process, a progressive series of reconciliations that:

1. Accommodates the individual manager's goals and plans to the personal needs and capabilities of subordinates
2. Harmonizes the manager's objectives and improvement plans with those of colleagues in other functions with whom the manager relates
3. Meshes the manager's objectives with the needs and goals of his or her superior, and with the goals, policies, norms, and values of the total enterprise

When this process of reconciliation is used with sincerity and sensitivity, it can produce a set of minor goals that fit comfortably under the umbrella of total corporate purpose, yet are powerfully motivative to individual managers.

AN EVOLUTIONARY STEP

It is not my intention to offer management by contract as a revolutionary process of management; it represents rather another evolutionary step in the direction of the truly productive enterprise. Only the integration of its elements is new—the elements themselves, in one form or another, are in use in most progressive organizations. The total process has been employed on a limited basis with results that suggest it has genuine potential to enhance organizational effectiveness and improve productivity. Admittedly, these benefits have not been validated by rigorous quantitative testing on a large scale. My personal experience with the process, however, has convinced me beyond all doubt that it can produce tangible benefits substantially in excess of those produced by the conventional MBO program.

ACKNOWLEDGMENTS

To write a book on any subject is an act of ego, but one on business management must be approached with more than a touch of humility. What can one add to what has already been written with style, grace, and insight by Drucker, Odiorne, McGregor, Toffler, Likert, Morrisey, Batten, Koontz, Jay, and many others? One can, however, construct a new tower upon an edifice built by others. Each of these writers and practitioners before me has built a major portion of the structure on which my concept is erected. Each has my sincere gratitude for his contribution to this work and to my management education. I have tried to acknowledge each individual source; if I have inadvertently failed to do so, I can only plead unintentional plagiarism.

I am also indebted to a great many people I have been associated with in business during the past 30 years or so. I would like to think that I have contributed something to them in return for the knowledge, insights, and viewpoints they have shared with me. There is no way I can list them all, but among them are Harold Geneen, Rich Bennett, Jim Rice, Hanford Willard, Gerry Andlinger, Murray Kirkwood, Earl Hilburn, R. J. "Steve" Saulnier, Joseph Hatchwell, George Scharffenberger, and George Haufler.

Several earlier influences on me are no longer in this world, but they are not forgotten. Among these are Colonel Sosthenes Behn, founder of International Telephone, General William Henry Harrison, who succeeded Behn, and Henry C. (Joe) Roemer, who surely was destined to lead ITT to great heights had he not died prematurely. At a very early time of my business career, Richard S. Bicknell taught me never to take anything at face value; it was he I observed checking the result on his Friden calculator with his pocket slide rule.

This book is affectionately dedicated to my wife, Helen, whose patience and support helped to make it possible.

Charles R. Macdonald

MBO CAN WORK !

MANAGEMENT IN A CHANGING WORLD

*The accomplishments of management past are acknowledged;
the failures of management present to recognize
and respond to the changing needs and
values of society are cited; and
the obligations of management
future to become more
responsive and productive
in fulfilling these needs
are specified.*

**PART
ONE**

THE CHALLENGE
TO MANAGEMENT

As the decade of the 1980s—the ninth decade of our century—unfolds, it finds the economic, social, and political institutions of America and the world in disarray. The prospect is that they will get worse before they get better. As a consequence, American industry faces challenges of a nature and magnitude never before experienced by its management.

An economy and a lifestyle built upon a bountiful supply of cheap energy are threatened by shortages and skyrocketing energy costs. Deeply embedded inflation is causing severe misallocation of capital by corrupting management's capability to evaluate economic risk and reward, by distorting the accounting for costs and profitability, and by debasing management's ability to measure organizational performance. The rapidly shifting norms and needs of our increasingly fragmented society are undermining the stability of markets and industries. And the legislative and regulatory environments in which business functions have become so unpredictable that its managers scarcely know from one day to the next what is expected of them.

All this is coupled with a raging current of change—technological, cultural, and economic—so swift it gives little or no time to adapt, and "so powerful," says Alvin Toffler in *Future Shock*, "that it overturns our institutions, shifts our values, and shrivels our roots. . . ."[1]

Our ability to meet and manage these menacing issues of the eighties is crucial to the competitiveness of our free market system. Failure to cope with them could jeopardize the very survival of the nation. Unfortunately, the experience of the recent past offers scant assurance that management is either prepared or willing to provide the leadership needed to deal effectively with the problems and perils that threaten us.

At an earlier time we would have had less cause for concern—perhaps even grounds

**CHAPTER
ONE**

for confidence—because the achievements of professional management have until recently been one of the remarkable success stories of this century. Management has helped to bring about—indeed has been the driving force for—the extraordinary improvement in the well-being of humankind in this period. Most notably, the interval between World War II and the late 1960s witnessed unprecedented advances of management as a discipline, a body of organized knowledge, and a profession. Seemingly no task was too great, no project too vast, for management to undertake and accomplish.

During these 2 decades or so, with a resplendent outburst of innovation and energy, American industrial management created a brand new world. The U.S. gross national product soared to over $1 trillion as a virtual cornucopia of consumer and industrial products poured out of U.S. factories. The skies of the globe were dominated by passenger aircraft bearing the label "made in America." United States automobile assembly lines were the envy of the entire world—and the pattern that Japan and Germany followed as they rebuilt their war-torn industrial economies. American accomplishments in space enthralled the free world. And American management methods were eagerly adopted as the standards for the industrialized world.

As the decade of the "soaring sixties" gave way to the "sagging seventies," however, a degree of disillusionment set in. As our institutions have increased in scale and complexity and the environments in which they function have become more turbulent, cracks have appeared in the management facade. The role of management has come under increasing scrutiny—and we may now be in a period of reflection and reconsideration of what management really is, and what its role in society should be.

In a number of important respects, management has failed in recent years to live up to its high promise and has fallen short of the expectations it has created. As a consequence, business as an institution and management as a profession have suffered a serious erosion of public confidence and a corresponding loss of power to attract the resources needed to accomplish demanding social tasks.

Management, in brief, seems to be experiencing an identity crisis

LOST CREDIBILITY AND LOST POWER

Because business has apparently failed to respond to certain basic needs of society, other institutions have gathered power and taken over the task. Government is now setting standards for the quality, safety, and performance of products—some unrealistically high, some with unrealistic target dates for compliance. These standards are causing severe disruption in the economy and are diverting massive amounts of capital from other uses. Government is also establishing, in its clumsy, heavy-handed manner, requirements for employee safety on the job, for the content of foods, for medication and health care, and for environmental protection—because business management seemingly has failed to respond effectively to society's demands for protection of workers, unadulterated food to eat, affordable health care, clean air to breathe, pure water to drink, and a planet free of chemical contamination.

Despite years of clear and unmistakable warnings that the major sources of energy are becoming less available to us, industry has continued to waste energy as though there were no tomorrow, and has failed to develop acceptable alternative sources that can be controlled. Industry has continued to produce millions of overweight and overpowered vehicles and thousands of energy-wasteful buildings, even while the technology to make them energy efficient is available.

Industry has turned its back on the decaying cities of the Northeast and the distressed areas of Appalachia—saying that social problems are not a concern of business—then has berated big government for taking away management's prerogative to locate its facilities where and when it chooses. By consistently failing to heed the economic storm warnings, and pursuing policies of expansion well into recession periods—then overreacting with massive cutbacks in capital expenditures, new product development, and marketing activities—industry has compounded the economic problem and given government a clear opening to take over more of management's obligations.

U.S. business firms show an increasing aversion to risk—preferring to service existing markets rather than to create new ones, imitating rather than innovating, looking for short-run returns, and acquiring existing businesses instead of developing new products themselves. Management has continued to consider its primary function to be that of maximizing profit, despite an overwhelming body of evidence that short-term profit maximization as an operating philosophy leads to excesses that lead, in turn, to business failure.

While politicians rush into the media to castigate business for its every transgression and "unconscionable" profits, management has been failing to tell its side of the story in a straightforward and credible way that the public will accept. Instead, business has continued to employ public relations flackery, long discredited in the minds of the public. Apparently in fear that stock values on the exchanges will drop, companies continue to report earnings per share that are distorted and bloated by inflation. As a consequence, the public and the Congress accuse the business community of "unpatriotic" capitalism. Unfortunately, every objection by business to ill-conceived, badly framed, poorly administered government legislation and regulation is viewed as a grievance. The reluctance of business management to challenge the constraints imposed by government at all levels leads to further inroads on its ability to manage.

Management has tended to misuse and underuse its human resources, all the while lamenting that productivity is low because "people just don't want to work anymore," despite evidence that most people will respond with honest effort and high output given clear goals, forceful leadership, genuine respect, and fair treatment. Top management continues to confuse personal aggression and assertive behavior with competence, and assigns resources to individuals who demand them, not necessarily to the ones who can utilize them most productively. Activity is often mistaken for accomplishment, with the consequence that the company reward system is skewed to the task instead of the result, and corporate internal defense mechanisms use up energies that could be better employed for productive purposes.

As a consequence, a high degree of discontent and a serious measure of alienation exist among middle managers. A recent national survey of middle managers indicates that, as a class, this important group of managers feel themselves to be powerless, seriously lacking in authority, and left out of the corporate decision-making process. They believe themselves to be less informed and less respected than the groups above and below them in the corporate hierarchy, and they believe that top management is unresponsive to their needs and problems. As a result, they identify less with the mission and goals of the enterprise.

THE HIGH COST OF FAILURE

Management tends to focus attention on problems, weaknesses, and deficiencies caused by its earlier failure to plan; accordingly, yesterday's mistakes consume its energies today, while the opportunities that will sustain us in the future remain unexploited.

The ineffectiveness of management in recent years is imposing a high cost on the nation's economy—in terms of opportunities not exploited through failure to plan, opportunities lost through bureaucratic lethargy, and opportunities mishandled because of failure to delegate decision-making authority. The insolvencies and bankruptcies that are reported daily are merely the surface symptoms of a deeper malaise. Massive losses and erosion of capital are not the result of deceit, dishonesty, and fraud, but of well-intentioned management that is failing to plan, to control, to delegate, to make hard decisions. The largest losses are the unrecorded ones—the difference between what is and what could have been had the opportunities been seized and exploited at the right time.

Management is failing through disregard for the real purpose of the business enterprise, which is to fulfill *needs*. This is the most basic of all the management fundamentals. This factor alone may be the key to improving the productivity of management.

The "quality of life" issue that has been taken up as a rallying call by the liberals in economics and politics has been distorted into a demand that management restore to society something it once possessed but has now lost in the rush to materialism. Despite the anguished cries of the nostalgia peddlers, however, humankind has never enjoyed a life free from pollution, poverty, squalor and crowding, unequal distribution of wealth and privilege, fear, and suffering. That it ever did so is a myth. Today's middle-class person would be appalled by the living and working conditions of the typical urban dweller and the remote farm family in the early 1900s. What society is seeking are *new entitlements*, born in large part of expectations created by management's own earlier accomplishments. What were once only unexpressed desires and wistful hopes have now become *needs* to be fulfilled.

Fulfilling these needs is the task of management, a task that calls for a resurgence of entrepreneurial spirit in managers. The voice of the entrepreneur, the innovator, is becoming lost in the labyrinth of the contemporary organization, whether business, social, or governmental. Efforts of managers are increasingly directed toward protecting gains already made, toward defending the company's resources rather than shifting them into more productive uses. The large corporate structure, with its legions of staff specialists and layers of organization, tends to spin a protective cocoon around its top management, isolating it from the discomforts of the outside environment, from the changing marketplace, from *customers*—who tend more often than not to be fickle, unpredictable, unreasonable, illogical, contrary, and demanding. Market research is often conducted in the conference room, where it can be done much more tidily, free from the distractions of the real world—and where it usually confirms management's conviction that the products and services the company is presently producing are the products the market needs most.

THE TRUE ROLE OF THE ENTREPRENEUR

Many entrepreneurial managers, to their dismay, find their efforts to force top management attention to the changing needs of people increasingly frustrated. Therefore, they break away from the establishment to create new companies and new industries: as Robert Noyce did when he left Fairchild Camera to develop the electronic marvel of the 1970s, the microprocessor (and built Intel Corporation into a $150 million business); as Gene Amdahl did when IBM rejected his proposal to create a new supercomputer; and as Fred Smith did when he built Federal Express from a vision into a major force in distribution. Unfortunately, every time an entrepreneur departs the corporation, some of its vitality goes as well.

The corporation tends to view the entrepreneur as a gambler, a high roller, even as a predator within its ranks—one who seeks to wrest control of the company's resources away from those appointed to guard them. The true role of the *entrepreneur*, as one who directs resources from less productive into more productive investments and thereby creates wealth, has been forgotten. Most firms were single-product organizations when the early English economist, Edwin Cannan, defined the function of the entrepreneur thusly:

> The power of managing industry is attributed not to the mute and inanimate capital, nor even to the owners of capital, but to *the entrepreneur ... who directs industry into particular channels by virtue of the orders of the consumer*, whose demands must be satisfied on pain of bankruptcy.[2]

This conception of the entrepreneur's role as the one who responds to consumer's changing needs is still valid—even in an age of multimarket, multiproduct, multitechnology, multinational, multibillion-dollar corporations. Only when the entrepreneur is correctly perceived as *a manager who anticipates needs and seeks the resources to fulfill them*, only when management recognizes that a continuous shifting of internal resources is a necessary condition for meeting market needs, and only when the corporate structure is redesigned to accommodate the entrepreneurial manager will the entrepreneur find his or her place in the corporation and the organization become truly productive.

THE ENTREPRENEURIAL ORGANIZATION

The challenge to management is to create the *entrepreneurial organization:* to direct every function, every department, every transaction, and every manager toward making every resource of the enterprise more productive in the terms that really count—fulfilling economic and social needs. These are not simply the needs of customers for utility provided by the goods and services the organization produces, but psychological and emotional needs as well; not just the needs of the owners and lenders for enhancement of their capital, but the needs of suppliers for profitable outlets for the products of their resources; not simply the needs of employees for money income, but their need for purposeful employment of their energies and capabilities. Additionally, the "new" needs of society must be met—with products that are safe for the user and the consumer, with production processes that are harmless to the environment and to workers, and with management policies and practices that provide truly equal opportunity for all.

These needs are imperatives, not options, for management. They are essential to the very survival of the enterprise. Failure to meet them will result, inevitably and inexorably, in the demise of the business enterprise. *Failure of the company's products to provide utility* will cause users to turn to others for satisfaction of their needs. *Failure of management to compensate all employees justly and equitably,* to employ their capabilities fully, to encourage their development as individuals, and to treat them with regard for personal worth and esteem, will cause them to withhold the physical and intellectual energies without which the enterprise will founder. *Failure of the enterprise to generate sufficient earnings* to pay the going rate of return will cause owners and lenders to put their capital to more productive uses. *Failure of the firm to deal fairly and honestly with suppliers* of materials and services will cause them to seek more desirable outlets for the output of their facilities. Finally, *failure of the firm's management to provide safe and healthful working conditions* for all employees, to produce goods that are free from harmful effects to the user, to avoid damaging the environment now and for the future, to husband all depleting resources, and to support nonbusiness institutions that provide essential services to society will cause loss of public support for business as an institution and, in the extreme, pressures for politicization and nationalization of private enterprise.

The challenge to management can be met only by improving the productivity of the entire enterprise in fulfilling these needs. This involves much more than the productivity of production workers in terms of output per worker-hour—it requires improving the productivity of every level of management. It demands improved productivity from the managers, technicians, administrators, and knowledge workers who form an increasing proportion of the firm's total human resource. For if improved productivity is to continue to be "the chief means whereby humankind can raise itself from poverty to a condition of relative affluence . . ."—in the words of productivity authority John W. Kendrick—we must heed him as he sums up a lifetime of productivity study with this advice:

> The individual producing organization is where the action is with regard to continuing productivity advance. Given the social and governmental backdrop, it is *the efficiency and innovativeness with which producing organizations are managed* that largely determines the rate of productivity advance in any economy.[3]

THE OBSOLESCENT ECONOMY

The challenges that confronted management in the past may come to seem almost trivial in comparison to those that lie ahead. It is becoming evident to some observers of the socioeconomic scene that the events which rocked the American economy during the past decade—the Arab oil embargo of 1973 and the Iranian crisis 6 years later—were only warning signals of even more ominous threats to our economic life. When the full impact of these and other traumatic events of the 1970s are finally felt, we may look back upon their initial shock as though they were minor rumblings preceding an earthquake. The reverberations that follow are certain to send massive shock waves through the entire industrial economy.

For it is increasingly clear that the energy crisis is causing violent and irreversible changes in the production, distribution, and ownership of goods in this and other industrialized countries. The implications are disturbing in the extreme—the changing economics of energy may require nothing less than total rebuilding of America's capital stock within this decade.

The task is a staggering one, and it clearly belongs to management. The dramatic surge in energy costs—arising out of the sudden recognition that even while the beginnings of the petroleum era are still fresh in our memory, its end is already in sight—has had the effect of making obsolete virtually every energy-using product in use today. To cope with this prospect will require the replacement or upgrading of every building, every vehicle, every power-consuming apparatus, and every industrial process designed and produced in the period of cheap and "plentiful" energy. The magnitude of the task is almost beyond belief—it calls for the replacement of more than 150 million vehicles with designs that are fuel-efficient, the energy upgrading of some 75 million housing units and millions of commercial and industrial buildings, the redesign and replacement of electric appliances numbering in the hundreds of millions, the replacement of countless engines, motors, control devices, lights and lighting fixtures, and the virtual revamping of our transportation systems. In short, it will require massive changes in everything that produces or uses heat, light, power, and motion.

A business organization that fails to take this massive discontinuity into account in strategic planning for the firm does so under peril of corporate obsolescence.

The nation's automotive industry was first to feel the effects of changing energy economics, and it is desperately undergoing a massive reorientation to energy-efficient output—at enormous cost. The new demands for energy efficiency come on top of the disruption caused earlier by the air pollution and passenger safety issues that imposed enormous capital expenditures upon the industry. Detroit's failure to heed the signals sent by the Arabs in 1973 has created problems the industry will suffer from for years to come, not least of which is a federal government presence in the boardroom.

The American steel producers, locked into processes designed in an age when first cost was the most important cost, are begging the Japanese to share their newer technology to make steel with less energy per ton. Producers of other commodities that rely on plentiful and inexpensive energy—aluminum, glass, and petrochemicals among them—are intensely restudying their processes for savings. Hospitals, already impacted by rising costs of labor and supplies, are faced with enormous expenditures to upgrade their facilities, which have been found to be extremely wasteful of energy. Colleges and universities are becoming alarmed about the excessive amounts of energy required to operate their obsolete physical plants; meanwhile they're raising tuition rates to unheard-of levels to help offset these high energy costs, effectively reducing enrollments and thus compounding the problem.

Home-heating contractors are inundated with orders from distressed homeowners to convert their furnaces from oil to lower-priced natural gas. Homeowners are also taking some tentative steps to make their houses more energy-efficient, with attic insulation, for instance—but much more remains to be done. Still ahead is the enormous job of upgrading and weatherizing America's aging housing stock—notoriously wasteful of energy. A recent study concluded that home energy conservation is the nation's least costly "source" of energy; roughly equivalent, they say, to discovering crude oil priced at $10 a barrel. It is sad that the industry that should be addressing this problem—the home-improvement industry—is hopelessly fragmented, undercapitalized, and inefficient, and shows little evidence that it is even aware a problem exists.

As energy costs continue to escalate, industry is demanding the redesign of every energy-inefficient, environment-polluting, high-cost industrial process in order to contain manufacturing costs. The situation will also require the redesign and retooling of virtually every electric and gas appliance to ever-higher energy efficiency ratings, along with redesign of the plants that produce them. The replacement of millions of obsolete machine tools together with the task of equipping newly designed production processes will place heavy demands upon the machine-tool industry, already backed up as much as 18 months.

Competitive forces will cause the laggards in this process to lose business to the more progressive firms with a marked cost advantage. Now that the energy crisis has turned the economics topsy-turvy, the initial cost of every energy-consuming product is more often the smallest part of the total cost—operating costs over the life of the product may be many times first cost. Less formidable, but still challenging, is the task of replacing countless numbers of electric motors and controls, gasoline engines, and lights and fixtures with new types that consume less energy per unit of output.

Bewildered power utility executives throughout the fifty states are seeking solutions to problems that have no apparent answers. Nuclear power will remain, for years to come, under the heavy cloud of fear and suspicion thrown up by Three Mile Island. The world is years of development and billions of dollars of capital investment away from synthetic fuels as a significant energy source. And the likelihood is small that some sudden breakthrough in technology or an unexpected discovery of major new sources of petroleum and natural gas will solve the dilemma. Direct power from sun, wind, and ocean tides will continue to be interesting possibilities, but will not be serious contributors to our energy resources during the lifetime of most of us. Nor is it credible to expect that conservation alone will bring relief. World energy consumption has tripled in less than a generation, from some 85 quadrillion Btu's a year in the mid-fifties to over 260 quadrillion today, and there is small possibility that growth of energy demand will greatly diminish, even given higher costs.

Ironically, the electric and gas utilities, whose profitability is tied to ever-increasing demand and consumption of energy, are the designated agency to spearhead the residential energy conservation program of the 1979 National Energy Act—an appointment that has been likened to "putting Dracula in charge of the blood bank."

OTHER JEOPARDIES AND THREATS

Accomplishment of the management task ahead, the rebuilding and resizing of the American industrial economy to cope with the new realities of energy, will impose staggering new demands for capital on our financial institutions—and some authorities question their ability to cope. The economy is already reeling from the government-mandated requirements for capital to control pollution, clean up the environment, and meet new standards for job safety and health, product quality, and product safety. The U.S. steel and automobile producers are expected to invest upwards of $110 billion in the next 5 years to recover their lost markets; GM alone plans new capital investment of $30 billion, double that of the previous 5 years. The problems are compounded by chronic embedded inflation, which is creating severe distortions and imbalances in all of our economic processes.

If American business management fails to rise to this challenge, it is certain that others will seize the opportunity to take a more active role in the U.S. marketplace. The Japanese steel and auto producers have already carved out a substantial share of the markets for their lower-priced steel and smaller, more fuel-efficient cars. Other foreign manufacturers are looking longingly at the huge American market.

A prospect with even more ominous overtones to U.S. industrial management is increased intrusion of government's heavy hand into the private sector. Failure of business to solve the problem will lead inevitably to more intervention by government, initially in the seemingly benign form of allocation of capital to those institutions that perform a "more useful social function." It is already happening. The National Energy Act of 1979 and the oil windfall profits tax are being used to divert capital in directions considered by government to be more socially beneficial. It may be that the road to nationalization of industry is even now being paved—and one of the signposts may read "Chrysler bailout."

THE CHALLENGE CAN BE MET

There is no intention here to offer a doomsday vision of the future. What is being discussed is going on right now; the possibilities presented are simply an extension to their logical conclusion of some trends that are already well formed. Others share in these views. Energy productivity authority Roger Sant of Carnegie-Mellon University has said that all of our equipment for converting energy into useful work is now old-fashioned relative to today's economics. Amitai Etzioni, director of the Center for Policy Research at Columbia University, has declared that nothing short of nationwide dedication to *reindustrialization* will restore the United States to its former prestige and competitiveness in world markets.

Nor is it intended to portray a situation without hope, or problems without practical solutions. The new task of management has its positive aspects. The energy crisis is creating as many opportunities as it is imposing threats. New occupations and new professional disciplines are being called for, and our educational institutions are responding to the demand. Energy managers are becoming members of top management in large decentralized organizations, responsible for improving energy productivity and controlling energy costs. New product lines are being created within existing firms, and entire new industries are being spawned to grow and displace those whose energy consumption cannot be curbed.

Management has met great challenges before, and there is reason to believe that management will not falter in this instance. Failure has too high a price tag—we simply cannot afford it. What is needed is a resurgence of entrepreneurial spirit throughout all of our institutions and greater dedication than ever before to the goal of improved productivity.

Every energy-producing and energy-consuming product and facility must become more productive—so too must every productive resource, every organization, every business function, and every manager. Both the threat and the opportunity demand it.

It is the intention and the hope that this book will make a contribution to the effort.

NOTES

[1] Toffler, Alvin, *Future Shock*, Random House, Inc., New York, 1970.

[2] Cannan, Edwin, *History of the Theories of Production and Distribution*, P.S. King and Son, London, 1903.

[3] Kendrick, John W., *Understanding Productivity*, The Johns Hopkins Press, Baltimore, 1977.

MANAGEMENT AND PRODUCTIVITY

THE STATE OF PRODUCTIVITY TODAY

During the past decade or so there has been a rising chorus of concern in this country that productivity has ceased to grow—that the engine which propelled the U.S. industrial economy to record heights of ouput and gave its population an enviable standard of living has run out of fuel. The consequences of this productivity lag (we are told) are high inflation coupled with high unemployment, erosion of our international competitiveness, and a slowdown in the growth rate of the economy. Unless the decline is checked (we are warned) it will lead to bankruptcy of our institutions, a reduced living standard for our citizens, and further maldistribution of wealth.

The severity of the situation has been described by one noted writer on productivity in almost apocalyptic terms, as a combination of circumstances that "could make the 1930s look like a moderate recession."

This decline in productivity of industry represents a reversal of the strong productivity growth trend which prevailed from the end of World War II to the mid-sixties. The slowdown is blamed on a number of complex and interrelated factors: among them, low rates of corporate capital investment, reduced government and industrial spending for research and development, a dramatic shift in the age/sex composition of the work force, and excessive and wasteful regulation of business by government. Some analysts blame the decline on a diversion of investment from "productive" uses to protection of the environment and the health and safety of workers.

Other causes cited by economic observers include the sharp rise in energy costs which has induced industry to employ expensive conservation methods, an increase in worker discontent and alienation from the establishment ("nobody wants to work any more!"), and a diminishing sense of enterprise and risk taking in the economy.

CHAPTER TWO

The statistics on productivity in the private domestic economy that are used to document these assertions tend to confirm that annual growth in output per worker-hour has slowed rather drastically: from an average of over 3.0 percent per year during the 15-year period 1950–1964, to about 2.0 percent in the subsequent 8 years, 1965–1972, to under 1.0 percent a year in the 1973–1979 period. Any reduction in the productivity of American industry, however slight, is cause for concern; the charge that the decline is leading us to economic disaster, however, may be overstating the case. Certainly basing the indictment upon a statistic that tells only part of the productivity story and ignoring other important contributory factors could lead to that suspicion. The politicians may well be using it to divert public attention from other serious causes of inflation and low economic growth for which government is accountable. Others may misuse it through lack of understanding of productivity concepts and the causes and consequences of changes in productivity. Edward Dennison, a productivity expert in the U.S. Commerce Department, states that many of the reasons for lagging productivity haven't even been identified. Productivity is not a simple matter, as attested by the large bibliography on the subject.

Output per worker-hour is just one of many measures of productivity, and only a partial measure at that. There is reason to believe that use of this single statistic is simplistic and potentially misleading. True productivity is defined in economic terms as the relationship between the output of all goods and services and the input of *all* resources, of which labor is only one; others are, of course, capital and natural resources. To use a single measure of productivity—output per worker-hour—as a basis for developing national policy or for formulating strategies to raise total output may be counterproductive, even dangerously so.

What may be worse, the data base on which the output per worker-hour statistics are founded is quite limited. Robert E. Sibson states that few companies actually measure their productivity. He reports the following:

> . . . based upon sample surveys, half the companies in the U.S. today cannot measure productivity anywhere in their operations. Half of those that *can* measure productivity anywhere *do not.* The few that do . . . have done so in only a few factories, offices, and field offices.[1]

PRODUCTIVITY OF THE HIGHER-LEVEL EMPLOYEE

It is possible that the concern about low productivity is misdirected. The core of the problem may be in the office, the technical laboratory, and the executive suite, rather than on the shop floor. Recent studies have indicated that productivity of higher-level employees—managers, administrators, technicians, and professionals—whose numbers are increasing rapidly, may be substantially below its potential. These studies have fixed a large share of the blame for low productivity in the workplace on management—because of unclear work assignments, improper staffing, inadequate communications, poor example setting, and lack of discipline.

Large business organizations are beginning to take a hard questioning look at the productivity of their higher-level employees—lawyers, accountants, bank lending officers, engineers, even scientists. They are finding it frustratingly difficult to get a handle on the problem; one compounded by the extreme reluctance of many professionals to be measured or graded. The conventional remedies for low productivity in the workplace do not seem to be effective when applied to knowledge workers. More often than not, they are resented—to the point where they are counterproductive. Clearly, new methods are needed.

At organization levels above the first-line supervisor, the terms "productivity" and "productivity improvement" are seldom used. Managers, technicians, administrators, and professionals tend to focus on input or activity rather than on output. When the term "results" is employed, it is seldom expressed in units of output but rather as the amount of activity performed. It is not uncommon to read activity reports that measure effectiveness in terms of days or dollars spent researching a market, worker-hours and money expended on an engineering development, number of meetings attended, number of sales reps hired, customers visited, or sales presentations made. Staff personnel, particularly those in control functions, tend to focus on controlling input and tend to become obsessed with allocating and restricting resources. Effectiveness in this instance is equated with expense budgets underspent, equipment purchases deferred or disallowed, personnel not hired, and projects not funded—often despite overwhelming evidence that the expenditure or the project is a more productive use of the company's resources.

Neither the amount of activity nor the control of input, regardless of the efficiency with which each is performed, can be considered productive—neither factor moves the enterprise toward its objectives. Clearly, to restrict the input of material to an assembly line worker in the name of economy would be counterproductive in the extreme, if not absurd. To do so would reduce production to the level of input, which the worker does not control, instead of letting the worker's skill and energy govern the worker's output. Yet this is precisely what is happening in offices, engineering departments, and technical laboratories when managers are denied the use of needed resources by self-appointed guardians of the firm's assets.

UNPRODUCTIVE PRACTICES OF MANAGEMENT

In the search for ways to improve the productivity of managers (the term as used here includes all people with management responsibilities: functional managers, administrators, technicians, professionals, and executives), it may be better to look inward at what is presently being done than to look outward for solutions to apply. There is evidence that the greatest gains in managerial productivity may come from the removal of unproductive practices and constraints that are inhibiting output. There are many of these in the contemporary organization.

The organizational structure can be a serious impediment to the full productivity of the firm. Most organizations, according to John Gardner, have a structure designed to solve problems that no longer exist. Other less apparent but nonetheless serious constraints are use of the conventional accounting system for management control reporting, a function for which it clearly was not intended; failure of managers to delegate effectively, either for protective or defensive reasons; lack of involvement in decision making by lower levels of management; and the traditional superior/subordinate relationship, a derivative of the hierarchical structure.

Most of these productivity impediments are heritages of an earlier, and simpler, industrial age. The hierarchy, unfortunately, is comfortable, and because it worked in earlier circumstances, it is retained. Antony Jay said that the hierarchical corporation tends to invest in "the qualities that brought it success in the past. Not only its management selection, but all its training and indoctrination are geared for *what used to work.*"[2]

Other organization customs can have a severe inhibiting effect upon productivity, among them the conventional chain of command, limited span of control, the single reporting relationship, and the sharp line/staff cleavage. These sacred cows roam freely through the halls of our institutions despite repeated demonstrations that an organization can slaughter them with impunity and gain enormously in management productivity.

Just as the rigid hierarchical structure can impede the free flow of information upward and downward, an inflexible compartmentalization of the functional organization restricts the informational flow between functions on the same level. These artificial barriers to intercommunication within and between organizational levels cause stagnation of information in functional pools. To be productive, information must move, must energize people, must compel action. Information that doesn't move ages fast, especially in a rapidly changing environment. Information that is a day old or a week old may be so out of phase with events that it has outlived its usefulness. Managers soon sense this and begin to suspect all information— suspicion leads to doubt, doubt to uncertainty, and uncertainty to inaction. In the extreme, the organization reaches a condition of stasis and equilibrium, and Le Chatelier's law of dynamics can take effect. Steel and Kucker observed that this law has an analogy to the bureaucratic organization in that each attempt by a manager to produce a change for the better creates counterforces that tend to drive the system back to its original condition, thereby preserving the status quo. The destructive consequences of this in a rapidly changing world are obvious.

After all is said and done, however, the greatest single obstruction to high managerial productivity may reside within the manager himself. It is the persistent preoccupation with *input* or *activity*, rather than output, that inhibits productivity of the organization. All the productivity potential created by capital investment, by engineering technology, by all the good efforts of hardworking production people, can be dissipated and lost by managers who fail to apply this potential to the achievement of beneficial goals.

Many of the problems and failings of management in recent years can be traced back to this factor. Emphasis upon input or activity implies emphasis on the *present*, while concern with results implies emphasis on the *future*. And the true productivity of managers is realized only when they address themselves to the future. The past cannot be changed; the present has been largely shaped by decisions already made; only the future can be altered to make it more productive.

INPUT, ACTIVITY, AND OUTPUT

A shift of emphasis from input and activity to *output* can have the effect of redirecting the energies of people from performing tasks to accomplishing results. Every worker, whether production line assembler, computer programmer, or chief executive officer, deals with the three factors of input, activity (or process), and output. There are no exceptions. Input is what each receives, activity is what each adds, output is what each produces. The output of each then becomes input to the succeeding transaction or activity. The assembler receives piece parts plus information (instructions), adds his or her manual skills and effort to put the parts together, then the assembler's output moves on to the next production stage or to storage. The programmer receives data plus information (specifications), and adds his or her analytical skills to produce software that enables the computer to perform a repetitive task. The executive receives information, and adds his or her intellectual skills to produce a decision that causes action on the part of people within the organization.

Schematically:

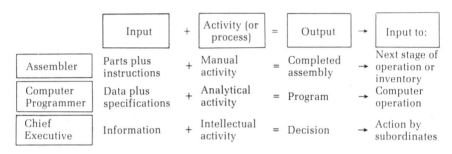

	Input	+	Activity (or process)	=	Output	→	Input to:
Assembler	Parts plus instructions	+	Manual activity	=	Completed assembly	→	Next stage of operation or inventory
Computer Programmer	Data plus specifications	+	Analytical activity	=	Program	→	Computer operation
Chief Executive	Information	+	Intellectual activity	=	Decision	→	Action by subordinates

PRODUCTIVITY AND QUALITY

Obviously, the quality of the input each receives is critical to the final output. The application of high work skill to flawed input is unproductive in the extreme. Recognition of this fact has led to important productivity gains in manufacturing, and to an important management discipline called *quality assurance*. It was common before World War II to observe rows of inspectors at the end of a production process, busily measuring, counting, and checking the output of the process—and rejecting many defective products *after* processing. With the development of quality assurance, the emphasis shifted radically from control of output (final inspection) to control of input, in which the defect is detected or corrected *before* the material moves on to the next stage of the process. Obviously, there is much more to quality assurance than this, but it is at this stage that the big payoff in savings and productivity improvement has been realized.

The philosophy applies equally to service industries, particularly to communications and information processing. Less frequently now is heard the expression that was once common in data processing, GIGO, which stands for "garbage in, garbage out." It was recognized that the speed and capacity of the modern computer is such that a little garbage in can result in a great deal of garbage out, so the industry has spent great sums of money to develop software and devices to check input to the computer for validity and accuracy— that is, to stop the garbage from getting in.

So has the communications services industry. Western Union, for instance, invested well over $1 billion during the years from 1964 to 1975 to convert its obsolete electromechanical telegram switching plant into the world's most modern electronic message communications network. During the same period the company invested many millions more to assure that incoming messages would be recorded accurately before handing them off to the transmission network.

Once the message is committed to the transmission system, a combination of error-checking equipment and software ensures its integrity through the system to its destination. But if the initial input is incorrect, no electronic black box is intelligent enough to correct a misspelled name, an incorrect street address, or a transposed number in the body of the message. Recognizing that correct input is a major determinant of quality output, Earl Hilburn, president of Western Union, ordered construction of a network of central telephone recording bureaus equipped with the most up-to-date electronic recording and editing equipment to ensure the accuracy of input.

IMPROVING MANAGERIAL PRODUCTIVITY

In conventional industrial engineering, the most striking productivity gains have resulted from improving the activity, or process. This is done by changing the method (often eliminating unnecessary steps in the process) and/or by mechanizing the process. These basic principles are also applicable to increasing productivity of managers and knowledge workers. The computer, of course, is the most visible of the machines that can improve managerial productivity (that it does not always do so is the fault of humans, not of the machine). As computers become smaller, cheaper, and more reliable, they will help management become even more productive. Unquestionably, the hand-held electronic calculator has increased managerial output, and the microprocessor will amplify it enormously. Communications devices that move information from point to point more rapidly, that can handle record communications, that have broadcast capability, and that can collect as well as disseminate information offer great potential for productivity improvement of knowledge workers.

The ubiquitous copier may have replaced the water cooler as the office gossip center, yet it has extended managers' capabilities to disseminate information remarkably. It will soon be teamed up with communications satellites to permit remote copying of multipage documents in many locations simultaneously (whether *this* will be a real advance for civilization remains to be seen).

Other important machines for enhancing managerial productivity are video cassette recorders for training, word-processing equipment, variable-speed audio playback units for "speed-listening," and audiovisual projection devices for conveying information rapidly to groups of people. All of these deal with symbols, words, concepts—the raw materials of knowledge workers.

It may be that greater gains in productivity in the managerial area will be realized from methods improvements than from mechanization. Conventionally, the production worker's output is increased by devising improved work methods, simplifying the process, setting standards of performance, documenting them, measuring actual output versus standard, and analyzing variances for corrective action.

It is not inconceivable that the productivity of the contemporary manager, technician, and professional can be enhanced through the application of a similar process.

It may be argued that we are not dealing with repetitive, manual operations; that the knowledge worker is a different creature than the production worker; and that tasks involving ideas, symbols, words, and numbers cannot be proceduralized, standardized, and measured. Sibson, for example, expressed the view that the application of scientific work methods to higher levels of management has a negative effect on productivity—that it is often the antithesis of effective work in many middle-level positions. Even Peter Drucker, who has probably done more to increase managerial productivity than any other individual, confesses to inability to answer what productivity is with respect to the knowledge worker, although he gives us a few important clues in this statement:

> There are few things as useless and unproductive as the engineering department which with great dispatch, industry, and elegance turns out the drawings for an unsalable product. Productivity with respect to the knowledge worker is, in other words, primarily quality.
>
> One thing is clear: making the knowledge worker productive will bring about changes in job structure, careers, and organizations as drastic as those which resulted in the factory from the application of scientific management to manual work.[3]

MANAGEMENT AND THE
ESSENTIAL DIFFERENCE

The difference between manager and production worker may be more of degree than of kind, and the differences are narrowing. If the job of the typical manager, technician, administrator, knowledge specialist, even the scientist or chief executive, is analyzed, it will be found to consist mostly of elements that are repetitive, predictable, and even routine. As few as one-fourth or one-third of the tasks can be classified as nonstandard. What is more predictable in a contemporary manager's day, for example, than that management decisions will be made and tasks will be assigned; that reports will be written and reports will be read; and that meetings will be scheduled and held? What is more certain than that plans of some kind will be written, reviewed, and amended; that progress against these plans will be monitored and reported; that budgets will be developed and performance compared with them; that new projects will be scheduled and controlled; that problems will be studied and solutions proposed; and that managers will communicate with one another and work together toward common ends?

Making a decision is a task. Writing a report and reading a report are tasks. Planning and conducting meetings, preparing and reviewing program plans, scheduling and controlling new projects—all are tasks. So are communicating with people and solving problems. Every one of these "tasks" contains elements that can be methodized. Standards can be set, procedures can be documented, output can be measured and evaluated—and productivity can be increased. This will not be done, we hasten to add, by some new breed of management industrial engineer, *but by managers themselves.* This, then, is the essential difference—the characteristic that Drucker refers to in a concluding paragraph to the statement just quoted:

> For it is abundantly clear that knowledge cannot be productive unless the knowledge worker finds out who he is himself, what kind of work he is fitted for, and how he works best. There can be no divorce of planning from doing in knowledge work. On the contrary, the knowledge worker must be able to plan himself.

This may well be the essence of his classic concept of management by objectives and self-control—the discipline known as MBO.

NOTES

[1] Sibson, Robert E., *Increasing Employee Productivity,* AMACOM, a division of American Management Associations, New York, 1976, p. 48.

[2] Jay, Antony, *Management and Machiavelli,* Holt, Rinehart and Winston, Inc., New York, 1967.

[3] Drucker, Peter, *Management,* Harper & Row Publishers, Inc., New York, 1974.

MANAGEMENT BY CONTRACT— MAKING MBO WORK

Management by objectives (MBO) is discussed as a concept with enormous potential for enhancing productivity of the business enterprise; its lackluster performance in practice, however, has raised concern about its value. The causes of MBO's failure to live up to its high promise are explored. The need for a higher order of self-management is cited, and a process called management by contract is offered as a method for making MBO work in an increasingly turbulent environment.

PART TWO

THE HIGH PROMISE
OF MBO

A management practice that has the potential to change the emphasis from activity to output, and to make the organization productive beyond imagining is management by objectives and self-control. Usually shortened to management by objectives, and popularly known as MBO, the discipline has been eagerly adopted and widely implemented during the past 25 years or so, with highly gratifying results.

Since Peter Drucker propounded the concept in the 1950s, hundreds of courses and seminars have been held to disseminate the principles and the techniques of MBO. Unquestionably, thousands of organizations and tens of thousands of managers have been drawn to its doctrines.

There was nothing new about managing by objectives when Drucker first discussed the practice in his 1954 book, *Practice of Management*. Some exceptional managers and a few exceptional companies had been managing by objectives for years. (George Odiorne has traced its origins as a concept back in time through Alfred Sloan and Machiavelli, to the Old Testament and the Koran.[1]) Drucker was simply displaying the insight and discernment that has marked his career as teacher, business consultant, and writer by identifying and labeling a method of managing that he had observed to be *the most productive* of all methods he had encountered.

Management by objectives is, in principle, a discipline that forces managers to set challenging goals for themselves and direct their efforts toward the accomplishment of these goals. When the goals and the efforts of all managers are in harmony with those of the total organization, the enterprise can achieve extraordinary results. When the objectives at the same time cause each manager to develop his or her potential to the fullest extent, then the process is rewarding to individuals as well as to the organization as a whole.

**CHAPTER
THREE**

In the conventional task-centered organization, individuals tend to become absorbed in the daily activities associated with a job to the point where they can lose sight of the job's real purpose. This is particularly prevalent among staff managers and professionals. A market research manager may, for example, begin to think of market surveys as an end in themselves, instead of seeing them as input to the process of setting marketing objectives and strategies and keeping these attuned to changing market conditions. A financial analyst may come to consider variance analysis as the primary purpose of the job, forgetting that the analysis is only a part of the feedback mechanism for controlling process costs.

Management by objectives has the potential to broaden the outlook of such managers—to give them a new awareness of the real purpose of their functions and a better appreciation of their individual contributions to the forward progress of the enterprise.

Many managers tend to become task-centered to the point where they seldom look beyond today's task to next week and next month; rarely do they look to next year. Every action taken and every decision made reflects this narrow focus and short time horizon. As a consequence of their failure to look ahead, these managers are frequently surprised by events and may spend most of their working hours in a constant state of crisis. MBO, properly used, can raise the sights of these managers and extend their time horizons by helping them to set objectives and develop improvement plans for an extended period of time ahead.

Some managers live in a tightly compartmented world doing their own thing with little regard for effects on people in other functions and with little awareness of their dependence upon others in the organization. The management by objectives process has the capability to lower the information barriers between functions and to stimulate productive communication between managers on different organizational levels.

Progressive human-resources people welcomed MBO because it gave promise of being the nearest thing to McGregor's "Theory Y" management style by providing a means by which to evaluate the performance and potential of people in less subjective, more "scientific" terms. Indeed, management by objectives as a management discipline has built a large and vocal following among academics, management consultants, and writers on management that is quite unique. The literature on the subject is growing rapidly and the discipline has found its way into nonbusiness institutions and government.

PROMISE AND DISAPPOINTMENT

Some of the global definitions found in the literature, however, cause one to wonder if MBO has not been oversold. MBO has been defined by various practitioners in these sweeping terms:

- A management system used to manage all human resources of the organization[2]
- A comprehensive entrepreneurial management control system[3]
- A means of controlling and implementing change . . . an antidote for "future shock"[4]
- A dynamic system which seeks to integrate a company's need to achieve its profit and growth goals with the manager's need to contribute and develop himself[5]
- A philosophy, a discipline, a style, a flexible response to differing pressures, . . . a *movement*[6]

Each of these descriptions contains a large measure of truth, to be sure, but they may have led to overexpectations. Inevitably, a reaction has set in. The effectiveness and benefits of MBO are now being critically examined and questioned—not only by its critics, as one might expect, but by its most loyal proponents. A number of definitive studies of MBO in the workplace have disclosed disappointing results, and in many cases, failure.

George Strauss has concluded, on the basis of a poll of a sizable group of companies, that only one-third of the firms which adopted MBO have retained it as a comprehensive managerial control system, while one-third eventually abandoned it (the remaining one-third applied it with mixed results).[7] Shuster and Kindall's later survey of the Fortune 500 largest industrials reported somewhat less favorable results; of the 120 firms which had tried MBO, only 10 percent considered that they had a successful application.[8]

MBO has its devil's advocates and critics, to be sure, and their labels for the practice run the derogatory gamut from "a great management illusion," to "snake oil for contemporary organizational medicine shows." Some critical observers have warned that MBO's excessive formalization can lead to alienation of managers and a preoccupation with form rather than substance—even, in the extreme, to reinforcement of bureaucracy in the organization. Management in France has tended to reject MBO as a threat to the prerogatives of top executives' individual decision making.

Most management authorities, however, share the belief and optimism of MBO proponent George Odiorne that use of MBO will continue to grow. Odiorne, one of the first, and certainly one of the most energetic of MBO advocates, has published several books and countless articles on the practice. He recently analyzed a number of applications in industry in a study entitled "MBO in the 1980's; Will It Survive?".[9] His conclusion is that MBO has achieved worthwhile results in those aspects of business management where the goals are financial and can be readily quantified. Where goals are nonfinancial in nature, there has been a tendency for things to slide back into older, more traditional modes of control. In the less tangible areas of participative management and others that require a behavioral orientation, MBO has not brought about much improvement.

Factors that have inhibited greater gains from use of MBO are given as:

- Resistance to change, for all the familiar reasons
- Tendency of creative marketing and engineering types to resist being committed to firm objectives and to shift goals with each bit of new professional knowledge they acquire
- Apparent inability to make MBO work in the organization as a practical management technique and discipline

Odiorne's assessment has led him to conclude that management has much to do and a long way to go before the promise of MBO will be realized. "There remains," he says, "a whole backlog of expectations that has not been fulfilled." Nevertheless he believes that pressures to improve the functional effectiveness of the organization will inevitably force wider use of the process. "The costs of failure are becoming higher," he states, "and the charismatic, intuitive manager's days are numbered."

The gap between the high promise of management by objectives and its lackluster performance in many situations is disturbing to other MBO proponents as well, although many of them share Odiorne's confidence that time and experience will eventually prove its value.

SELF-CONTROL, THE MISSING ELEMENT

A clue to the disappointing performance of MBO might be found by going back to Drucker's original expression of the concept—management by objectives *and self-control*. The second part, self-control, seems to have been lost or mislaid in the intervening 25 years, yet it may well be that MBO cannot succeed fully without it. As Drucker says, "one of the major contributions of management by objectives is that it enables us to substitute management by self-control for management by domination." He goes on to say that of the hundreds of companies that have adopted MBO, "only a few have followed through with true self-control."[10]

Self-control requires more than mere involvement in the process through which objectives are developed. Studies of MBO by Carroll and Tosi in a large progressive firm indicate that participation in goal setting will not result in better response to MBO unless such participation is part of the superior's typical management style. "To have any impact," they say, "participation in goal-setting must be part of a more general overall managerial style consistent with mutual goal-setting. The subordinate must be given the opportunity *to participate meaningfully in more than setting goals.*"[11]

Drucker confirms that managers must go beyond mere participation—that they must take an active and responsible part in defining the needs of the organization and developing objectives directed toward fulfilling them. He has suggested that a very effective way to accomplish this is through the medium of a "manager's letter."[12] This is described as a process in which managers define in writing the objectives of their own jobs and those of their superiors *as they perceive them.* They then set down the performance standards they believe are being applied to them. Next the managers list the things they must do to attain these goals, as well as the things within their own units that they consider to be major obstacles. They then list the things the superior and the company must do to help them. Finally, the managers outline what they propose to do during the next year to reach their goals. After approval, these statements become "job charters" by which managers measure and *control their own performance* during the ensuing period.

Clearly, self-control for a manager involves a great deal more than simply controlling one's own job performance. What is called for is a larger process of *self-management*—a process that involves the design of the job itself. This process must begin early, with an evaluation of the job, the function, and organizational ambiance, and then move onward from this base to the setting of objectives. The act of self-appraisal is an important element of the process presented in this book. This is discussed at length in later chapters.

MBO FAILURE—OR MANAGEMENT FAILURE?

If management by objectives is not succeeding in organizations where it has been adopted with high expectations and implemented with enthusiasm, either the process is structured improperly or the programs are not being administered effectively. If neither of these is true, the conceptual soundness of MBO itself must be questioned.

The conventional management by objectives program (if the term "conventional" can be applied to a discipline so young) starts with establishment of objectives for the total organization. In a typical producing organization, these include objectives for volume and profitability, market penetration, new-product innovation, utilization of resources, and productivity improvement—all of which can be quantified. Other more qualitative goals may be set, as well. Normally, these objectives are developed at a high level of the organization. Objectives are then fed back down through the chain of command, or announced in meetings, to lower-level managers for their guidance in developing their individual objectives.

Each manager then prepares a listing of key tasks and sets performance standards for each. The resulting document may be called a Key Results Analysis, or something similar. The manager then develops a short-term improvement plan designed to correct deficiencies, to raise performance levels, and to support topical company programs. These are thereupon discussed with the boss, who either approves them or directs the manager to modify them. Some contemporary programs require the manager's boss to approve the Key Results Analysis and the improvement plans of the manager's direct subordinates, as well.

Typically, the MBO process calls for a periodic review of the manager's actual performance by the supervisor, at which time the Key Results Analysis is updated and a new improvement plan is prepared. Concurrent with the performance review, a so-called "potential appraisal" may be made. Less frequently, a salary review may be conducted at the same time. In schematic form, the process is deceptively simple (see Figure 3.1).

Figure 3.1 THE MBO PROCESS

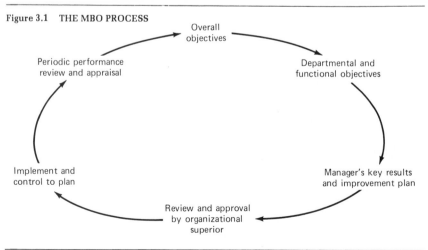

Often associated with the MBO program is the management development process of training, job grading, compensation planning, and management-succession planning. In theory, these processes should combine to move the firm forward and cause it to achieve its objectives. At the same time, managers are enabled to develop more fully their own potential as individuals. That it doesn't always work this way has led to disenchantment with MBO in recent years, to the point that it has been branded in some organizations as a failure.

What, if anything, is wrong with this process? Why isn't MBO living up to its high promise?

PRODUCTIVITY AND MBO

The literature on management by objectives offers many definitions of MBO, ranging from a "form of participative management" to a "comprehensive management system." It is possible, of course, for a discipline as comprehensive as MBO to perform several functions. At the same time, the wide range of definitions and the lack of a single overriding purpose may have led some practitioners to view it as a panacea for every corporate ill. Fortunately there is a common thread running through the fabric of every MBO study—*the improvement of managerial productivity*. The answers we seek, therefore, should be sought within this context; the process should be examined to determine:

1. What elements it may lack that are critical to improving productivity
2. What elements it contains that may be unproductive or counterproductive

Several points quickly become apparent. First, some MBO programs lack a systematic, disciplined approach to the setting of functional objectives. There appears to be a belief that manager and subordinate can simply sit down at the beginning of each period and talk until agreement on job goals is reached. Yet there is evidence that such agreement may be quite rare in practice. Odiorne, for example, cites research[13] which concludes that, typically, superior and subordinate tend to agree on about 75 percent of expected outputs on regular, ongoing activities and on about 50 percent of the subordinate's major problems; but the superior agrees with no more than 10 percent of the subordinate's ideas on how the job of the subordinate can be improved. In effect, this says that the boss will *disagree with the subordinate's objectives 90 percent of the time*. The chances are quite low that a subordinate can overcome such unfavorable odds—in most cases, probably, the boss cuts the discussion short by setting the goals unilaterally and arbitrarily.

What is missing from this process is a firm methodology for building a foundation of facts, hard numbers, and organized information which will enable the manager to present and defend the goals with vigor and confidence, and upon which can be erected a structure of objectives sturdy enough to withstand the forces of external change and internal job pressures.

Second, great emphasis is given to the preparation of a Key Task Analysis—a job description by another name— leaving little time for developing improvement plans of the sort that represent real progress for the function. One well-regarded book on MBO dismisses improvement plans in a single paragraph.

Yet if objectives are the motivating power that moves the enterprise forward, the vehicle must be the improvement plan. (In some programs there is not a clear distinction between plans and objectives—they are totally different things and must be treated as such by functional managers.)

Third, conventional MBO programs appear to be too little concerned with an important aspect of management productivity, the close and continuing interaction among managers in different functions. Surely to a functional manager who is part of an integrated operation, the goals and plans of colleagues must be of more than passing importance. A free and open interchange and discussion of these among managers during the process can do much to tear down the barriers between functions and make the total organization more productive. There is awareness of this deficiency—West German industry management, for instance, has adopted a variant of MBO called "management by joint goal setting." Also it has been reported that Rensis Likert is preparing a book on management by group objectives.

Related to this is a rather serious lack of functional coverage in some programs. In most firms of any size, there are a number of activities that cross conventional functional lines to become "everyone's concern but no one's responsibility." Customer service, housekeeping, and more recently, energy conservation are among these. The MBO program must recognize these as functions for which objectives must be set, improvement plans developed, and progress reported.

Fourth, most MBO programs continue to treat the manager's organizational superior as the dispenser of reward and punishment and the sole judge of performance. It is the boss, more often than not, who actually sets the manager's objectives. In some cases, this approval power extends to the objectives of the manager's subordinates as well—thus the boss can override their supervisor and set their goals too. As one authoritative text puts it, "the superior must, of course, retain the right to have his way."[14] What is lacking is some affirmation of the superior's responsibility to lead, support, and guide the manager toward the objectives—as well as to provide the resources needed. That the boss will always do this cannot simply be taken for granted; the process should hold the superior accountable when a goal is missed because the manager lacked a critical resource, or because the supervisor failed to provide support at a critical point in a project.

Related to this is the leadership style of the superior and its effect on the superior/subordinate relationship. For a boss to leave a manager on his or her own when the task is new and unfamiliar to that subordinate represents failure to lead. Just as clearly, for the boss to closely supervise a task that the manager has performed well many times before is equally poor leadership. The lack of a clear and governing leadership requirement tailored to particular tasks can lead to one or both situations. Simply to assume that every superior will provide the right degree of leadership in every situation is unrealistic in the extreme.

Next, an element that is missing from some MBO programs is a disciplined, formal system of reporting progress toward objectives. Progress is invariably made in small increments; progress is made day by day, week by week, month by month—it doesn't occur all at once just at the time of the quarterly performance review. An effective MBO system must demand that each manager report progress at frequent intervals—not for the boss's sake, but for the manager's own control. Lack of this discipline may be the most serious deficiency in MBO, because without it there can be no self-control—and without self-control, management by objectives is a hollow shell without substance.

Sixth, the use of MBO for narrow purposes only, such as for performance appraisal, for example, may be one of the common causes of failure. It is acknowledged by serious students of management that the performance review is the most sensitive aspect of MBO and the factor that can make or break a program. McGregor recognized this early and warned against the superior placing himself "in the untenable position of judging the personal worth of subordinates."[15] When programs lack a broad company charter, they tend to become dominated by the personnel function, at times to the detriment of the larger, companywide purposes of the programs. Douglas Sherwin counsels caution in basing performance appraisals on the results of MBO objectives alone, and Mobley reports that AT&T is moving away from MBO as a device for appraising subordinates. Apparently there are doubts about the performance appraisal as conventionally perceived and administered and doubts about its role as a contributor to the productivity of the organization.

At the other extreme, use of MBO for the sole purpose of achieving company objectives, at the sacrifice of the personal aspirations of managers, can be antithetic—even destructive— to productivity.

Finally, some MBO programs seem to be based in large part upon executive exhortations to excel, appeals to managers' company spirit, and inspirational calls for improved performance. Much of this is unproductive, especially when programs lack methodology and structure. All the good intentions and enthusiasm in the world will accomplish little without a system and a discipline to convert them into personal commitment and a firm plan of action. (Conversely, the finest system devised will fail if managers lack interest and strong desire to contribute.)

CAN MBO LIVE UP TO ITS PROMISE?

This analysis leads to the question, Can management by objectives be structured in a way to make it live up to its billing as a "comprehensive entrepreneurial management control system"? Can the productive qualities it lacks be restored, and can its nonproductive aspects be cast out?

Larger questions loom: Is MBO worth saving? Is the concept still valid and applicable to the contemporary corporation? Has the experience of some 25 years confirmed its soundness, or has experience cast doubt on its viability? Is it possible that events have passed it by since it was first proposed?

Personal experience with management by objectives programs in several corporations, discussions with the top executives of more than sixty progressive firms, and a review of the management literature for the past 15 years or more have led this writer to conclude that the concept of management by objectives is valid— more so today, perhaps, than at any time in the past. *But it is valid only when it is firmly coupled with genuine self-control.* This requires that the authoritarian subordinate/superior relationship be profoundly altered. Until this relationship is restructured into one in which there is *genuine sharing of responsibility for performing tasks, credit for accomplishment,* and *accountability for failure,* MBO will fail to achieve its enormous potential for productivity improvement.

MBO AS NEGOTIATED CONTRACT
BETWEEN SUBORDINATE AND SUPERIOR

Is it possible to bring about a change in relationship as profound and as radical as this? Can it be done within the existing structure of organization? What will it take to accomplish it?

There is a way—and the way has been pointed out in several important studies of MBO. Drucker was first, of course, with his "manager's letter," which represented a written commitment by the manager to perform stated tasks designed to produce a desired objective. Several writers since have alluded to the *contractual nature* of MBO, Villareal among them. In his stimulating article "MBO Revisited," he observes that MBO represents in many ways a contractual relationship and recommends that "all goals and measurements be stated in writing and all concerned individuals agree by affixing their signatures, in a fashion similar to a legal contract."[16]

Earlier, Phil Scheid described a "charter of accountability," which went beyond the manager's letter to become a form of contract between manager and boss. The charter consists of (1) a statement of job purpose, (2) a listing of objectives, (3) a breakdown of functional responsibilities, and (4) a subseries of performance tasks which provide the manager with definitive targets toward which to direct his or her specialized efforts.[17]

Some of these have tended to be somewhat one-directional, however, focusing on the obligations of the manager to the organizational superior, as though assuming that the boss will always fulfill the obligations to subordinates in an exemplary manner. Paul Hersey and Kenneth H. Blanchard[18] saw the problem in two dimensions; they recommend that manager and superior jointly negotiate a "psychological contract" clearly defining the role of the leader and the style of leadership desired and needed for the accomplishment of objectives. They point out that a boss may have to employ a variety of leadership styles depending on the subordinate's maturity in relation to each task. Thus, a task for which the subordinate admittedly lacks sufficient technical skill and know-how may call for a style characterized as "high-task" (direct explanation and detailed instruction) and "high-relationship" (continuing contact, communications, facilitation, and emotional support by the boss). In this instance, close supervision will be perceived as nonthreatening.

Where the subordinate has exhibited a high degree of maturity, capability, and willingness to assume responsibility for results, a "low-task" and "low-relationship" style is called for. When this is agreed upon in advance and included in the psychological contract between manager and boss, infrequent contact is viewed as an indication of trust and confidence, not lack of interest, and therefore is perceived to be a positive rather than a negative reinforcer.

There is a clear implication in this proposition that MBO imposes a binding obligation on the manager's organizational superior as well as on the manager. Surely, to the extent that the achievement of an approved objective is dependent upon the utilization of resources not under the manager's control, the responsibility of the boss to provide these resources is clear. Failure to provide the resources is to share in accountability for failure to accomplish the objective.

George Morrisey, who has taken the MBO concept a step further by giving it a more explicit description—management by objectives and results—has suggested that manager and superior both should have copies of the negotiated MBO agreement and use it as a basis for regular joint reviews of performance and progress toward objectives.[19] It seems clear from this that Morrisey views the output of the dialogue between the two parties as a form of "contract"—a document that serves to validate and make binding the mutual understanding that has been reached.

THE CONTRACTUAL RELATIONSHIP

This book takes this concept a step further and structures a system of *management by objectives, self-appraisal,* and *self-management* which takes the form of a negotiated contract between each manager and his or her superior. The contract represents the manager's commitment to carry out an action program directed toward achieving a set of agreed-upon goals within a prescribed time frame; the quid pro quo on the part of the boss is a commitment to provide the resources, leadership, guidance, and support needed to implement the action programs. The two are interdependent and neither is complete without the other.

The contract is binding upon the two parties. The manager's commitment is strong, because the objectives, performance standards, and improvement plans have been developed *by the manager himself,* based on a searching and methodical appraisal of the function or activity. Subsequent approval by the boss results from a process of face-to-face negotiation and agreement between the two on the priorities of the goals, the action plans designed to achieve them, and the resources and support required to carry them out. The supervisor's commitment is equally strong, because of intensive participation in the process as well as dependence on subordinates to accomplish the goals that he or she has contracted for.

Managers having one or more persons reporting to them have two contractual relationships governing their activities. The first is the contract with each subordinate to provide the resources, leadership, and support needed to meet their jointly defined objectives. The second is the contract with their organizational superiors to carry out, within time and cost schedules, the improvement plans to which they have agreed. The process can go all the way up to the chief executive's office and down into the organization as far as the first-line supervisor. There is an upper limit, of course, but there is no reason other than administrative constraints to set a lower limit.

The process will be called *management by contract* throughout this book. The contract itself may be called a "performance" contract, an "objectives" contract, a "management" contract, or an "MBO" contract. Its principles and general mode of operation are described in the next chapter. Detailed procedures for implementing the program, together with required forms, are given in subsequent chapters.

NOTES

[1] Odiorne, George, "MBO: A Backward Glance," *Business Horizons*, October 1978.

[2] Lea, G. Robert, "An MBO Program For All Levels," *S.A.M. Advanced Management Journal*, Spring 1977.

[3] Strauss, George, "MBO: A Critical View," *Training and Development Journal*, April 1972.

[4] Odiorne, George, "MBO: Antidote for Future Shock," *Personnel Journal*, April 1974.

[5] Humble, John W., *How to Manage by Objectives*, AMACOM, a division of American Management Associations, New York, 1972.

[6] Hives, Peter, "The MBO Movement," *Management by Objectives*, Vol. 1, Number 1, Fall 1971.

[7] Strauss, George, "MBO: A Critical View," *Training and Development Journal*, April 1972.

[8] Shuster, Fred, and Kindall, Alva F., "Where We Stand Today, a Survey of the Fortune 500," *Human Resource Management*, Spring 1974.

[9] Odiorne, George, "MBO in the 1980's; Will It Survive?," *AMA Management Review*, July 1977. (New York; AMACOM, a division of American Management Associations.)

[10] Drucker, Peter, *Management*, Harper & Row Publishers, Inc., New York, 1974.

[11] Carroll, Steven J., Jr., and Tosi, Henry L., *MBO: Applications and Research*, The Macmillan Company, New York, 1973.

[12] Drucker, Peter, op. cit.

[13] Odiorne, George, *MBO II*, Fearon-Pitman Publishing Co., Belmont, California, 1979.

[14] Humble, John W., op. cit.

[15] McGregor, Douglas, *The Human Side of Enterprise*, McGraw-Hill Book Company, New York, 1960.

[16] Villareal, John J., "MBO Revisited," *S.A.M. Advanced Management Journal.* (New York: Society for Advancement of Management, April 1974.)

[17] Scheid, Phil N., "Charter of Accountability for Executives," *Harvard Business Review*, June/July 1965.

[18] Hersey, Paul, and Blanchard, Kenneth H., "What's Missing in MBO," *Management Review*, October 1977. (New York: AMACOM, a division of American Management Associations.)

[19] Morrisey, George L., "Making MBO Work," *Training and Development Journal*, February 1976.

WHY MANAGEMENT BY CONTRACT?

Management by contract is a management process that combines the most productive elements of management by objectives and self-control (MBO) with several added ingredients. The most important of these is a formal contract between the manager and the organizational superior. Other added ingredients are a structured self-appraisal of the manager's function, formal progress reporting, and a structured system of internal and external control reporting.

The setting of functional objectives and the development of improvement plans are carried over from conventional MBO, as is the preparation of updated position descriptions. In the process of integrating these elements into the management by contract system, each has been modified for the purpose of making the total system more effective in improving managerial productivity.

FUNCTION OF THE CONTRACT

The *contract* is an agreement that spells out the respective roles, relationships, tasks, and responsibilities of both managers and supervisors. It represents a formalizing of the commitments of each individual to the other and to the organization as a whole. It provides for a *more equitable sharing of responsibility for results, credit for accomplishment,* and *accountability for failure.* It is the element that has been lacking in the MBO process, the added ingredient that has the potential to reenergize the process wherever it has been tried and failed, the element that can help to make it work in organizations that have not yet tried MBO.

Addition of the formal contract to the process in an organization that already has a generally effective MBO process is only a small step administratively, although it may represent an enormous leap in terms of philosophic acceptance by some

CHAPTER FOUR

managers of profoundly altered relations with their organizational superiors, with their subordinates, with the organization of which they are a part, and with their own jobs. One of MBO's distinguishing features, and one of its primary strengths, is its requirement for a high level of maturity on the part of each manager. *Management by contract demands an even higher degree of maturity in each of these relationships.* The process, in fact, is designed to foster and develop such maturity—not overnight, to be sure, but through successive iterations of the process.

THE CHANGE OF RELATIONSHIPS

In the case of the first relationship, the manager no longer looks to the boss as a source of authority and command but rather as a provider of resources, guidance, leadership, and support. The manager's relation with subordinates becomes one in which the manager assumes full responsibility for subordinates' results and shares fully in accountability for their failures to achieve objectives—while at the same time accepting that they must be given the opportunity to control their own interim results.

In terms of relations with the organization, the "bureaupathic" manager who functions solely by regulations and rules of order may find that these no longer operate to provide the psychological security this type of person seeks. *The contract can restore some of this lost security.* It must be recognized, however, that this type of manager may be unable to adapt readily to the new management style.

The manager's relationship with his or her job may be even more radically altered by this change in the process of management, from a focus on input or activity to one that recognizes and rewards only results; a massive shift in job concept from means to ends. The emotional dislocation that this can cause to some managers has been a serious obstacle to the successful implementation of MBO in a number of organizations. The contract can serve to lessen the manager's trauma by providing assurance that the organizational superior shares responsibility for achieving the stated objectives.

The management contract, like any contract between two parties, involves a sharing of responsibility for performance. The boss cannot withhold resources or support without sharing in accountability for failure. Nor can the superior impose new tasks and objectives upon subordinates without assessing the impact upon their existing workloads and without considering the possible jeopardy to accomplishment of existing goals. The importance of this can hardly be overestimated. In their study of MBO in a large manufacturing firm, Carroll and Tosi found that more than 40 percent of the managers were concerned because, after the goals were set, their time had been preempted by higher management. This change was not noted on their review forms; accordingly they felt threatened.

The contract between manager and boss is a two-way agreement. The manager says, in effect, "here is what I am convinced needs to be done in order to make my function or activity more productive, both internally and in relation to the other functions. This is my committed contribution to the company's goals." The superior, by approving the goals and plans, says, "I agree that the objectives and priorities you have established are the ones that will make the greatest contribution to departmental and total company results." If not, they will negotiate and agree on changes. Secondly, the boss makes a commitment to provide the resources needed: money for operating expenses, facilities and equipment, personnel, and staff support. Additionally, the superior undertakes to act as intermediary for the manager with higher levels of management as may be necessary to get the job done.

This has the potential for creating a new kind of relationship between manager and supervisor. No longer are the two in strict superior/subordinate roles but rather in positions of mutual support and interdependence. The boss, having communicated the goals of subordinates upward in summary fashion, is dependent upon them for achievement—and must be equally committed to them. The manager now looks to the superior not for commands but for support, guidance, and leadership. It must be recognized that *if the committed support is not provided, the failure is a breach of contract by the superior;* inasmuch as the manager's goal accomplishment is based on this support, whenever it is withheld or withdrawn, the manager's commitment to the objective is no longer binding.

Control of the manager's activities now becomes, in larger measure, *self-management.* The manager alone needs to be concerned with current control information on performance, because the manager makes the control decisions based on previously approved action plans. The supervisor's main concern should be with progress and results, not interim efforts. The supervisor's interest in the control data should be only that it is valid and unbiased, and that it is utilized. It is not essential to see the data concurrently to make this judgment.

As a management process, management by contract is neither authoritative nor permissive, neither bottom-up nor top-down, but represents a dialogue between levels of management based on verifiable facts and conducted in a climate of mutual respect and regard for personal worth and esteem. It is a structured process of management in which human values are central.

THE ORGANIZATIONAL POWER SHIFT

The factor that makes the contract and the process feasible—one of the factors, indeed, that makes it necessary—is the pronounced shift of power that has taken place within the contemporary business enterprise. New power structures have evolved within the organization as a consequence of the evolution of society from the millenia-long agricultural economy to an industrial economy some two or three centuries ago—followed by a change to a rather fleeting and somewhat transitional "service economy" after the end of World War II, and more recently by a shift to an economy heavily based on knowledge and information, the *knowledge economy.*

During the agricultural period, and later during the industrial age, total authority and real power both resided with the owners of land and money capital. Workers of the land were powerless—even as the migrant farm workers are today. Factory workers possessed little more power, although they did gain some slight measure in the late nineteenth century through unionism. During the brief period of the so-called service economy—hardly more than a generation—there occurred a subtle downward shift of power to service employees. Because the nature of their work activities caused them to be in constant direct contact with the firm's customers, these employees gained significantly in their ability to influence decisions of the people in authority, through their more intimate knowledge of customers' real needs and desires. Because they often were remote from direct supervision by management, they were able to influence the profitability of the business through their attitudes and behavior—thereby gaining power from those in authority.

As one example, Western Union, a major communications service company for more than 100 years, was brought to the brink of disaster in the early 1960s through its failure to serve its customers effectively and profitably. The company's loss of capability to render accurate transmission and prompt delivery of high-priority telegrams to the public was a result, in large part, of poor employee attitudes toward authority and indifferent behavior toward customers. A new management has since corrected this situation through massive investments in mechanization coupled with a 60 percent reduction in the service work force.

IMPACT OF THE KNOWLEDGE ECONOMY

Currently the economy is undergoing a transition to a society in which all the food, all the goods, and all the services we need are produced by substantially less than half the working population—and the majority of employees deal daily with knowledge and information, in the form of words, numbers, symbols, and ideas. Even now, half of the total U.S. gross national product is produced by *information industries*—data processing and computers, printing and publishing, research and development, consulting, advertising, education, the graphic arts, and communications. Business investment is heavily slanted toward support for the knowledge employee rather than for production machinery.

Accompanying this economic sea change is a pronounced shift of power to employees who possess the knowledge and control the flow of company information to those in authority. Data-processing managers are a highly visible example of such. This reflects a disconnection between authority and power—illustrated by the schematic shown in Figure 4.1 (adapted from *The Brontosaurus Principle* by Dr. Thomas Connellan, management authority and director of the Achievement Institute of Ann Arbor, Michigan).[1]

Figure 4.1   SHIFTING POWER STRUCTURES

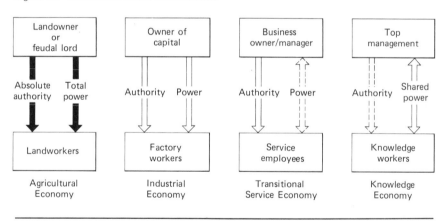

In this new power structure, real power resides in knowledge and information and can flow sideways or upward. The authoritarian hierarchy—the classic pyramid—remains the basic organizational form to be sure, but there is no longer any real "unity of command," in Herbert Simon's words. The 1978 Nobel Prize winner in economics has designated the new structure a "dynamic hierarchy," and has suggested that there are now two organizational hierarchies—an *administrative* hierarchy which is personnel-related and a *functional* one which is business-problem-related.[2] This has implications for the application of the management by contract process in the matrix organization.

IMPLICATIONS OF THE POWER SHIFT

Some years ago, Samuel Eilon defined power as the ability to affect a change in one's environment or in someone else's environment. This clearly implies ability to influence the decisions of others. As genuine power has moved downward in concert with the evolution to a knowledge-centered organization, upper management has been forced to acknowledge its increasing dependence upon lower-level knowledge workers for information upon which to base its decisions. For an example, marketing managers are becoming more and more conscious that their power is increasingly dependent on their market research staffs. For without up-to-date knowledge of market trends and developments to support their recommendations for marketing strategy, marketing managers may lack power to influence the decisions of the firm's general manager. To speed up the operational decision process, management is finding it necessary (and productive) to delegate day-to-day decision-making authority to these possessors of knowledge and information—and to increasingly redefine its own role to one of long-range planning, strategic objective setting, policy formulation, organizational development, and resource allocation.

This potent combination of power and delegated authority now invests lower-level managers with enhanced ability to influence the future course of the enterprise—accompanied, of course, by increased responsibility for results and a share in accountability for failure. A consequence of this development is the need for the functional manager to take the initiative in setting objectives for the function or activity; not to wait passively for the organizational superior (who may lack specialized knowledge and information) to establish these goals. This implies an upward flow of objective setting and a significant upward orientation for the whole MBO process.

This power shift is a non-zero-sum game; all manager-players win. It does not represent a loss of power by the superior. True, subordinates gain power to make more of their own decisions and to influence the decisions of others, but there is no lessening of the power of the boss. There is no diminution of the superior's strength to reward and withhold reward, no loss of effectiveness or productive capacity. Rather, the superior gains through enhanced capability to command the carrying out of many actions with a single directive; to set into motion a whole series of productive tasks simply by ratifying subordinates' objectives and improvement plans. What is more, through expanded capacity to produce—to direct the activities of subordinates to the accomplishment of gainful objectives with less expenditure of time and effort—the superior gains immeasurably in capability to achieve results.

THE "LINKING PIN" MANAGER

The transition to a knowledge-based enterprise serves to reinforce the role of functional managers as the "linking pins" of the organization. Increasingly, knowledge and information are the links. Rensis Likert, director emeritus of the Institute for Social Research at the University of Michigan, developed the linking pin theory—now considered a classical concept of organization—some 20 years ago.[3] In his conception of the organization as structured groups of people whose purpose is the accomplishment of work, each manager acts to link his or her work group to the next higher and the next lower organization levels.

Figure 4.2   RENSIS LIKERT'S LINKING PIN CONCEPT

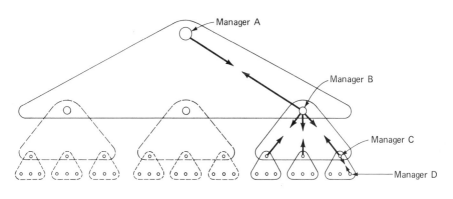

In the stylized organization depicted in Figure 4.2, manager B links his or her work group with the higher group headed by manager A. Manager B also links to the lower work group headed by subordinate manager C. In the management by contract process, manager B has a contractual relationship with both boss A and subordinate C. Manager B's contract with superior A is to direct the work group toward accomplishment of an improvement plan which involves the group; Manager B's responsibility to subordinate C is to provide resources and support to the work group headed by C as required to meet the agreed goals.

In this light, the MBO contract can be seen as something more than an agreement between individual managers. It can represent a contractual arrangement by a superior for the performance of work by a *work group* headed by a subordinate manager. Conversely, it can represent a commitment by the individual members of that work group to strive toward a group objective. This has the potential to foster a heightened sense of group purpose and shared mission—a new spirit of community—within the organization. The contract in this context provides an opportunity and a means by which to measure group performance, and to recognize and reward outstanding group achievement.

Manager B also shares responsibility to ensure that the objectives of all three work groups are not only compatible but reinforce each other. The peer reviews and the contract negotiations discussed in later chapters help to provide this assurance.

NEED FOR THE CONTRACT

It is not the intention of the contract to add a legal dimension to the manager/superior relationship, nor is it intended to protect the rights of one or both parties within the corporate structure of rules and regulations. This contract is *not* an employment contract, nor is it a compensation contract. Accomplishment of demanding objectives should be rewarded, of course, by compensation, by recognition, or by promotion, but these rewards are dependent upon other factors as well, so should be kept apart from this contract. The paramount purpose of the contract between superior and subordinate is to promote genuine delegation of authority and to create a more equitable sharing of responsibility for results, credit for accomplishment, and accountability for failure. When such a formal document spelling out the obligations of each to the overall organization as well as to one another is lacking, it is all too easy for a manager to take credit for subordinates' accomplishments and to avoid criticism for failure by shifting the blame to the performance of subordinates.

It must be emphasized, however, that a contract cannot impose upon a manager a binding obligation to achieve the objective. Such an agreement would be manifestly unfair and unworkable. An objective is an expression of intention—a desired end result. Obviously, no manager should be put in the position of guaranteeing an end result, given the uncertainties and unknowns of the future. What *is* imposed upon the manager by the contract is the responsibility to carry out, within the time and cost constraints specified and to the best of his or her ability, the improvement plan contained in the contract.

The improvement plan is a vital part of the contract, and an important element in the whole process. It is the element that translates objectives into actions designed to accomplish them. When a manager falls short of objectives because of failure to follow the plan, that manager has failed to live up to the agreement. When, on the other hand, the manager follows the plan in spirit—with proper regard for changes in situation and recognition of new opportunities—and still falls short, then the commitment to both superior and the organization has been fulfilled.

When the subordinate manager has a firm, documented plan of action approved and endorsed by the boss, the subordinate is in a better position to resist the many pressures that would preempt time and divert resources away from the central objectives. When the boss has agreed in writing to provide the resources and support that both have agreed are necessary to accomplishment of objectives, it is unlikely that these resources will be withdrawn or withheld for specious or frivolous reasons.

The contract serves as a management mechanism to formalize the task and performance requirements and the working relationships negotiated between manager and superior. The resulting document will guide and govern the actions and the interactions of both, without lessening initiative on the part of either. The contract also makes firm and binding the commitment to perform the many demanding management tasks of gathering and sorting data, analyzing and organizing information, selecting from alternative problem solutions, and documenting plans—tasks that often are given low priority. The essential output of the functional organization is, of course, customer orders on the books, reliable goods and services produced and delivered, positive cash flow, and a high return on the money invested in facilities, working capital, and people. The planning and documentation are important, as well, because they provide assurance that the company's business is conducted on the basis of current and factual knowledge of markets, prospects and customers, competitors, environmental conditions, and internal capabilities and resources. They also provide the company with definitive plans to exploit opportunities and to cope with adversities.

The management by contract process has the potential to raise the performance standards and productivity of the organization successively at each annual iteration. It can assist managers at all levels to better visualize and understand their respective roles and functions within the total organization's purposes and objectives and can help to make their individual contributions more effective.

The process can help to control and stabilize the organization in the face of change. The forced discipline of looking constantly toward the future, of anticipating change and developing plans to cope with it, can create a management structure capable of absorbing the shocks and strains of external events and developments without injury to the organization. Additionally, the process has the potential to convert the sometimes destructive tensions and conflicts between managers of different functions and at different levels of the organization into productive forces, and to substantially improve the interworking and coordination among the many functions of the business.

NEW DEMANDS ON THE
DELEGATION PROCESS

During the current decade of the 1980s, a remarkable change is taking place in the composition of the U.S. population—a change that is profoundly and irreversibly affecting the way that our institutions (business organizations in particular) are managed. The ability of our established institutions to cope with and capitalize on this demographic change is critical to our long-term future.

During the 1980s an enormous increase is occurring in the most dynamic element of our population, as the famous postwar "baby crop" comes of age. "Comes of age," that is, in terms of taking its place in productive society. The number of people in the age group from 30 to 45 years will have grown by 1990 to 60 million from only 36 million in 1975, an astonishing 67 percent increase in only 15 years.

On the basis of evidence to date, this population group is sure to be characterized by better education, greater mobility in jobs and living, higher expectations, and highly individualized lifestyles. The group is also marked by a degree of cynicism and a distaste for authoritarian structure. In business, individual members tend to be far less committed to a particular organization and to exhibit less allegiance to a specific company or industry. Their loyalties seem to be oriented to a profession instead, and their commitment is to the task, the challenge, or the problem. They are seeking meaning and purpose along with financial reward.

This remarkable group of young managers and professionals is rapidly moving into positions of authority and responsibility in commerce and industry, bringing with it a different set of personal goals and aspirations that are certain to have an effect on business management. For one, the nature of their jobs is becoming less and less related to a specific product, to a specific company, or even to a specific industry, giving them far more options and choices of association (and far less need to stay in a situation which fails to provide them satisfaction—one of these options, in fact, is to drop out of the establishment with much less penalty than in the past).

Among this group are a great number of women. The trend is already strong. In 1979, according to the Association of MBA Executives, women accounted for nearly 20 percent of the MBAs produced by America's graduate schools of business administration. These talented people are bringing with them into the management ranks a unique set of needs and aspirations to be fulfilled.

"Business must change," says Alvin Toffler in Future Shock, "in order not to alienate this important group."[4] One of the changes that top management must make to accommodate these achieving men and women is to shift increasing amounts of authority, power, and responsibility to them. Failure to do so will cause the enterprise to lose the enormous energy, drive, and intelligence that this group possesses.

The top-down authoritarian mode of management must surely give way to a more equitable distribution, a diffusion of power throughout the organization. This does not require a radical redesign of the hierarchical structure; it does, however, call for a significant and basic alteration of the process of managing organizations of people in the pursuit of excellence. Management by contract has the potential to draw this dynamic and highly achievement-oriented group of people into the management process. By assuring these managers a more constructive role in the setting of the goals of the enterprise and genuine participation in the organization's decision making, the process can cause them to contribute more fully and more energetically to these goals. And by providing these people the opportunity to control their own interim efforts as they work toward goals to which they are committed, the enterprise can attract and hold the most productive and valuable members of this group. This in no way implies permissiveness, or license for managers to "do their own thing" without consideration for the larger needs and goals of groups of which they are an integral part.

ALLOCATION OF RESOURCES

In real life, resources are always limited, and the process of allocating them is the heart of any economic system. Competition for resources is a necessary element of the allocation process, whether it is competition between corporations in the investment capital markets, between divisions of a company for shares of fixed and working capital, or between functional departments and project managers for operating funds.

One thing is certain—if resources are *not* limited, they are not being used efficiently. Whenever a corporation, a division, a department, or a project has a surplus of resources, then to the degree these resources are unutilized, the organization is unproductive. The effective allocation, and the perpetual reallocation, of resources, therefore, is an essential element of productivity. Resources, in economic theory, are allocated to those who promise to use them most efficiently and productively. There is always an element of the future in this regard, and consequently a degree of risk. (When the promise is not kept, of course, the resources should be withdrawn and reallocated.) There is also an element of the past, in that a history of superior performance in utilizing resources by a business firm or an individual breeds confidence in the ability of that firm or person to manage them well in the future.

Another vital factor in this respect is the degree of commitment to productive goals on the part of the individual who seeks the resources—commitment to objectives that potentially will enhance the productivity of the total enterprise in fulfilling needs. Commitment is a key element of the process being presented—commitment that is all the more binding and substantial because it is first of all founded on a sound, factual base of self-appraisal and finally is documented and ratified in a contractual agreement.

Management by contract represents a further stage in the process of allocating resources to accomplish results. Conventionally, resources are allocated to departments or sections of the organization through the capital and expense budgeting process. The management by contract process can make possible the efficient reallocation of these resources downward to individual managers within a department or project, based on the effectiveness with which the resources will be employed to productive ends.

RELATIONSHIP TO OTHER MANAGEMENT PROGRAMS

The management by contract program does not displace other management control systems, such as budgeting and business planning, but rather acts as a useful supplement and a vital information input to them.

By forcing managers to think analytically about every aspect of their functions, to identify the critical factors that need strengthening, and to concentrate their management experience and skills on the high-priority tasks, the program takes on the characteristics of a job-enrichment program for managers at all levels. A highly beneficial fallout results from the need for individual managers to delegate authority for the less critical but still necessary decisions to subordinates. By so doing, these managers can reach out for additional responsibilities and thereby move upward in the organization.

Before these decisions can be delegated, however, the manager is forced to restructure tasks and set up measurements and controls to assure their proper performance. This is the manager's opportunity to carry the principles of management by objectives and self-control a step further by guiding subordinates in the performance of this restructuring.

The self-appraisal described later may be the element that has been missing from zero-base budgeting—the element that serves to anchor the budget development process to a base of hard, verifiable facts, the element that may make it work in organizations where it has been tried and has failed. The self-appraisal does not eliminate the need for internal auditors but rather permits them to concentrate their professional skills on the demanding tasks of validating and verifying procedures, controls, and data bases.

STRUCTURE—AND THE ENTREPRENEUR

Studies of MBO effectiveness in business and government organizations invariably point out the dangers of overcomplicating the program. Surveys such as the study of MBO in twenty-one organizations by Towers, Perrin, Forster and Crosby, and Carroll and Tosi's Black and Decker Manufacturing Company study indicate that one of the strongest objections to MBO in practice is excessive paperwork. Shaffer warns against "paper snowstorms"—and energy spent on mechanics rather than results. Babcock and Sorensen have observed that, whether we like it or not, MBO is an additional activity superimposed on managers' existing activities.

As a consequence, the literature is filled with advice to the newcomer to MBO to "keep the program simple." This conclusion is well intentioned, but may be misinterpreted to mean that an MBO program should be loose and unstructured. Indeed, a more certain formula for failure would be hard to find. Management by objectives has been defined as "systematic, formal goal setting and review conducted jointly by managers and subordinates throughout various levels of an organization." "Systematic and formal" implies structure. Structure requires specific written procedures and well-designed forms for goal setting and review. There is a prevalent misconception that formalizing and structuring a program creates rigidity and inflexibility. The opposite is more likely true. As Humble says, "a well-based plan with assumptions clearly stated and agreed upon is in fact a foundation for flexibility."[5] Furthermore, if MBO is to be integrated into the other management disciplines of strategic planning, operational planning, information systems, and management development, as Humble and others recommend, it requires organization and methodology. This implies procedures, measurements, analyses, and controls—in short, structure.

Odiorne provides a definition of MBO which clearly implies that the process must be a highly organized and structured one:

> ...a process whereby the superior and subordinate managers of an organization jointly identify its common goals, define each individual's major area of responsibility in terms of the results expected of him, and use these measures as guides for operating the unit and assessing the contribution of each of its members.[6]

To impose such a demanding management process upon an organization, even one of modest size, without a well-structured set of policies, rules, procedures, guiding instructions, checklists, schedules, and forms, is an invitation to management anarchy. It is unrealistic to expect that a process as rigorous and complex as this will be adopted and effectively employed by a diverse group of managers with differing personal aspirations and highly individual styles of managing, given only top management blessing and good intentions. The requirement that all members of an organization follow a uniform structure is not a demand for conformity. Structure doesn't mean rigidity and immutability. Originality and creativity are not necessarily suppressed by formal standard practices; properly conceived, these practices provide formats that encourage individual expression in substance. Giving every manager license to design the vehicle in which to convey objectives and action plans to higher management levels can only lead to chaos.

(Inevitably, of course, in any organization there will be a few mavericks who will resist using a uniform format and want to devise their own. It is better not to repress them but to learn from them— succeeding iterations of the MBO process may be better for it. One of the keys to MBO success is flexibility in application; the fact that the process is organized and structured doesn't imply that it must be applied mechanically, without regard for individual differences in circumstances and people.)

That the management by contract process is highly structured may seem to fly in the face of the contention made early in this book that the new challenge to management is to create the entrepreneurial organization. It may be thought that structure, discipline, and procedures are antithetical to the methods of the entrepreneur, who frequently flees the large corporation to avoid regimentation, paperwork, controls, and measurements.

On the contrary, structure, discipline, and standard procedures can encourage innovation—can foster the entrepreneurial spirit—provided that they are designed to encourage and promote self-management. The prevalent notion that entrepreneurs are takers of risk simply for the excitement of the gamble is a serious misconception. True entrepreneurs are perceivers of unfilled consumer needs, corporate "gadflies" who demand that company resources be freed up from unproductive uses and redirected to the purpose of fulfilling these needs. In the process, these nonconformists inevitably collide with the guardians of the firm's resources—the input-oriented managers who perceive as their purpose the *conservation of resources* rather than their utilization, the *prevention of change* rather than the productive use of change.

Entrepreneurs usually bolt from the corporate structure because they envision unfilled needs and are frustrated from filling them—not by paperwork but by narrow minds, not by procedures but by shortsighted management policies. Follow these mavericks as a new computer company is created, a new integrated circuit produced, a new communications service established, or a new publication launched—and see how quickly performance measurements, planning, standardized procedures, control reports, and structure are instituted to control the entrepreneurial organization productively.

An explicit case in point is Robert Noyce, chairman and CEO of Intel Corporation of Santa Clara, California. Noyce has twice defected from large corporations because of his entrepreneurial itch. He left Fairchild Camera and Instrument Corporation in 1968, together with a fellow scientist, to form a new semiconductor company. In a 1980 interview, Noyce told a *Harvard Business Review* editor about the management control programs he now uses to manage an organization of highly creative people. "It's a very disciplined organization," he stated. Strategic planning is embedded into the organization as a primary function of managers. "MBO is practiced all the way through" as a management discipline and as a communication mechanism between divisions, departments, and peer groups. Furthermore, Noyce said, "at Intel we measure absolutely everything we can in terms of performance."

When asked whether highly independent scientists and engineeers didn't resent being measured, he is quoted as saying, "High achievers love to be measured . . . otherwise they can't prove to themselves that they're achieving. The fact that you're measuring them says you do care. People have control of their own destiny and they get measured on it."[7]

Intel today is an envied market leader and technological innovator. Profit margins are double the industry average, and the firm is headed for an annual sales level of $1 billion.

NOTES

[1] Connellan, Thomas, *The Brontosaurus Principle*, Performance Press, Ann Arbor, Michigan.

[2] Simon, Herbert, Interview With Herbert Simon in the *AMA Management Review*, January 1979.

[3] Likert, Rensis, *New Patterns of Management*, McGraw-Hill Book Company, New York, 1961.

[4] Toffler, Alvin, *Future Shock*, Random House, Inc., New York, 1970.

[5] Humble, John W., *How to Manage by Objectives*, AMACOM, a division of American Management Associations, New York, 1973.

[6] Odiorne, George, *Management by Objectives*, Fearon-Pitman Publishing Co., Belmont, California, 1965.

[7] Reprinted by permission of *The Harvard Business Review*. Excerpt from "Creativity by the Numbers" interview with Robert N. Noyce (May-June 1980). Copyright by the President and Fellows of Harvard College; all rights reserved.

HOW TO MAKE MBO WORK

PRECONDITIONS FOR SUCCESSFUL MBO

Up to this point in the discussion, emphasis has been on establishing the need for an improved process to manage organizations of people for productive purposes. Recognition was made of the immense contribution that "management by objectives" has made to this end during the past 2 dozen years or so. To repeat, what MBO has done is generate a high degree of acceptance for the notion that *results are what count*; MBO has at the same time created a large reservoir of goodwill among achieving managers because it gives visibility to competence and promises to reward accomplishment.

The last chapter described a process designed to capitalize on this store of goodwill and acceptance. This process, called management by contract, builds upon a foundation of management by objectives a structure of individual self-controls and group coordination intended to make MBO live up to its promise as a practical management discipline for improving the productivity of the organization.

From this point onward, the discussion is directed to you, as a practicing manager in the real world of turmoil and change. The intent is to help you *make MBO work* in your job, in your function, and in your organization.

Virtually all authorities on management agree that the first condition for successful MBO is a hospitable and receptive corporate environment. George Odiorne has discussed this requirement in his books, *Management by Objectives* and *MBO-II*, and in articles such as "The Politics of Implementing MBO."[1] Richard Babcock and Peter F. Sorensen, Jr., recently provided a checklist for evaluating this situation in a July 1979 *AMA Management Review* article entitled "Are Conditions Right for Implementation?"

CHAPTER FIVE

The essential corporate conditions that are needed, it is agreed, are an internal environment that favors change, an open, nonthreatening atmosphere of trust, a willingness of those with authority to share it through delegation, and firm, visible, and unwavering support from the very top of the organization. There are other necessary conditions—perhaps the most critical is that corporate management actively pursues policies of modern personnel management, recognizing that the human resources of the enterprise are, in the final analysis, its most valuable and important resources. In this context, there must also be evidence of genuine acceptance within the organization of the principle that the majority of managers are mature, competent, and intelligent persons who will respond with energetic effort and high productivity when they are treated with respect and regard for personal worth.

This discussion presumes that all of these conditions obtain within your organization to a sufficient extent that this process is not doomed to fail from the start—as it inevitably will in any organization lacking these essential preconditions.

As a practical matter, it also presumes that the company already employs the conventional array of modern management methods—business planning, budgeting, and management control reporting—and that the firm is profitable and growing, although not as profitable, perhaps, and not as fast-growing as top management would prefer. Finally, it presumes that you, the reader, are a functional manager or professional who is sincerely desirous of improving your personal productivity and the productivity of your function. It is hoped that you can begin to apply the principles and practices offered here to make your own function more effective. It is hoped, as well, that you have aspirations to become a general manager in the future, because this methodology being described in these pages is an integrated process for managing all of the resources of the organization more productively.

PRODUCTIVITY IS THE PRODUCT
OF A PROCESS

The contract has been discussed as the physical embodiment of the agreement between you and your organizational superior; it has also been described as being symbolic of a changed relationship between you to one more reflective of a mutually beneficial partnership. But the contract is more than this; it is the centerpiece of an integrated process of management that has the potential to make the whole organization enormously productive.

The process begins with a penetrating and critical appraisal of each management function or activity, conducted by the managers of the functions themselves. Several other actions precede the preparation of the contract—and a number of important activities follow the signing of the document. Each of these steps is crucial to the process— none can be eliminated, and the sequence must be followed.

Management by contract is above all else a discipline—a structured process for improving the productivity of management. Each functional manager is required to perform a number of clearly defined tasks, or steps in the process, in a fixed sequence. *Each step is dependent upon the preceding one, and the output of each becomes the driving input to the subsequent step.* Frequent and close interchange of information with peer managers and others is built into the process—it is not an option with the manager. The output of the final task in the series—the product, in fact, of the entire process— is a set of new, higher productivity standards—standards that also serve as a springboard for the next annual iteration of the process.

To put the total process into perspective, the ten steps are first described briefly, followed by a highlight summary table (Table 5.1, pages 62–63) that lists the steps, their associated tasks, and the output of each step. It was pointed out earlier in the discussion on productivity that the true output of any task is its *input* to the succeeding task or transaction. Accordingly, in this table the output of each step in this process is expressed in terms of its input to the next step.

The table is followed in turn by a schematic (Figure 5.1, page 64) which depicts the circular nature of the process.

STEPS IN THE PROCESS

Step 1: Building a foundation of facts. Your first task is to conduct a searching self-appraisal of your function. An essential part of this task is gathering data and organizing it into information. You will be guided through this appraisal by a set of detailed checklists which cover the key aspects of functional management.

Step 2: Creating the challenge. Based on this critical evaluation of your functional strengths and weaknesses, you can now proceed to develop a set of proposed objectives designed to increase productivity of your function and enhance its contribution to the total organization. These are the principal goals that your function will work toward during the months ahead.

A secondary output of this step is a set of updated job descriptions which document the latest performance standards for all key tasks of the function.

Step 3: Translating goals into action. This task is one of programming your objectives—that is, developing improvement or action plans to achieve them. These plans will serve as your principal guide during the period ahead. During this stage, you should be involving your subordinates in the process. Also, during this stage you should be making some accommodations and concessions to *their* strengths and weaknesses, as well as to their personal development goals.

Step 4: Creating coordination with others. This is the critically important task of communicating your goals and plans to your peer managers in order to ensure compatibility of objectives and forward plans. At this point, you normally will make some adjustments and concessions to organizational harmony. Any remaining incompatibility will be carried forward to the negotiations with the boss for resolution.

Step 5: Getting your share of resources. This task is a complex one of initiating and conducting a dialogue with your superior about your proposed objectives and plans, and negotiating for the resources you believe are needed to accomplish them. Almost invariably, you will be required to amend your proposed goals in order to bring them into accordance with the needs and objectives of your boss. Usually your proposal will be amended, as well, to improve its compatibility with overall corporate goals, policies, and strategies and to resolve any potential conflicts or duplications of effort between managers.

Step 6: Documenting the agreement—the contract. This is the task of documenting the understanding between you and your boss on your respective roles and relationships during the period covered by your plans. In this step, a single document is prepared, summarizing the output of all preceding steps—your self-appraisal, objectives, and improvement plans; the results of your discussions with your subordinates and your peer managers; and the trade-offs you may have made during negotiation sessions with your boss.

The act of signing the document formalizes it into a *contract* between you and your superior.

Step 7: "Getting there" through controlled self-management. With the fact-finding and planning stages of your job completed, coordinated with others, approved, and converted into a document of understanding between you and your boss, you can move confidently into the "doing" aspects of the management task.

This is the implementation task, the carrying out of your plans to achieve your objectives, guided by the program task elements, time schedules, and cost estimates contained in your plans. Your main task during this phase is controlling functional activities through "feedback" reports that compare actual performance to milestone events in your plans.

Step 8: Coping with change. This is the task of dealing with events and developments that are certain to occur as you proceed to carry out your plans. These are of two varieties: one, the *adversities* that threaten to cause missed completion dates, cost overruns, and failed actions; and two, the *opportunities* to beat your plan schedules, save money, and improve your planned results. The medium you will use to keep informed about these threats and opportunities is the periodic control reports issued by the controller and other functions. Your adaptive mechanism is your periodic updating of the plan (in extreme cases, the contract may be modified).

Step 9: Getting credit for your gains. This is the task of reporting your own progress toward your objectives. Using the milestone events and cost estimates in your plans as benchmarks of progress, you should prepare weekly and monthly progress reports. These reports are one of the principal means for recording your gains. They are also the medium for keeping your boss (and others) informed about your progress, potential problems that may require executive intervention, and potential opportunities that may require a reallocation of resources. They are also a very useful vehicle for assuring that your accomplishments are made known to others.

Step 10: Closing the objectives gap. The objectives of the truly productive enterprise (or function) are never fully accomplished—because there is always a greater challenge. All you can hope to do is narrow the gap, by continually raising the performance standards of the organization and its every functional element. Step 10 is the task of anchoring your gains by documenting the new higher performance standards of your function that you have achieved through the preceding steps of the process.

This can be done by reviewing, at year-end, your monthly progress reports and recapping your function's major accomplishments and progress toward objectives. This final step of the process melds into the reiteration, the annual recycling, of the process—as you proceed to make a new functional self-appraisal as the basis for a new set of objectives for the period ahead.

Table 5.1 summarizes these ten steps in terms of their task elements and their input to the succeeding step.

TABLE 5.1 Ten Steps to Higher Productivity

Step	The Task	Responsibility for the Task	Output of the Task and Input to the Succeeding Step
1. Building a foundation of facts	Conduct functional self-appraisal	Each functional manager	A set of checklists containing a critical evaluation of functional strengths and weaknesses
2. Creating the challenge	Establish functional objectives for next 3, 6, and 12 months	Functional manager	A set of improvement goals toward which the function will work during the coming year (accompanied by updated position descriptions for all major functional tasks) Proposed leadership "style" desired for each major goal
3. Translating goals into action	Develop detailed functional improvement plans to implement the objectives	Functional manager—assisted by subordinates who report directly	A set of specific action steps to be taken, together with a schedule of time and costs, resources needed, benefits, and assignment of responsibility for each step
4. Creating coordination with others	Exchange objectives and improvement plans with peer managers, and discuss matters affecting their interrelations	All functional managers reporting to department head	Modifications to the initial set of objectives and improvement plans, intended to improve integration of functions. Identification of potential areas of conflict and duplication among the functions
5. Getting your share of resources	Review proposed contract together with proposals of other direct reports. Discuss and negotiate changes singly and jointly with others who report directly	Department head and subordinate managers	Objectives and improvement plans in close harmony with objectives of the department head and the overall goals of the organization Resolution of conflicting goals and plans between functions; elimination of duplications of effort; and assignment of responsibility for activities not covered

Step	Action	Responsibility	Output
6. Documenting the agreement—the contract	Agree on "management contract"	Manager and department head	A signed document of understanding that constitutes for the manager a set of specific tasks to accomplish and a set of time and cost schedules to meet; for the superior, a specification of the resources, support, and leadership he or she is obligated to provide to the manager
7. "Getting there" through controlled self-management	Implement the contract; that is, carry out the improvement plan to time and cost schedules	All managers and department head	Joint accomplishment of plans through coordinated efforts. High productivity and effective accomplishment of tasks. High quality functional output
8. Coping with change	Review control report and modify actions (if events signify, propose modifying the contract)	All managers and department head	Revised action plans (amended contract)
9. Getting credit for your gains	Prepare periodic progress reports (weekly and monthly)	All managers and department head	Factual reports of progress toward objectives; identification of problems for joint resolutions; identification of opportunities needing coordinated effort
10. Closing the objectives gap	Document new performance standards (based in large part on progress reports)	All managers	A record of higher productivity standards for performance of tasks, such as increased output, improved quality, and reduced costs

The process of management by contract is described in graphic form on the schematic diagram shown in Figure 5.1. Although it is depicted here in two dimensions, it might better be likened to an upward-spiraling stairway; each step takes you higher, and each circular iteration brings you back to the same point but on a higher level.

Figure 5.1   THE MANAGEMENT BY CONTRACT PROCESS AT THE OPERATING LEVEL
A Two-Dimensional View of a Three-Dimensional Management Process.

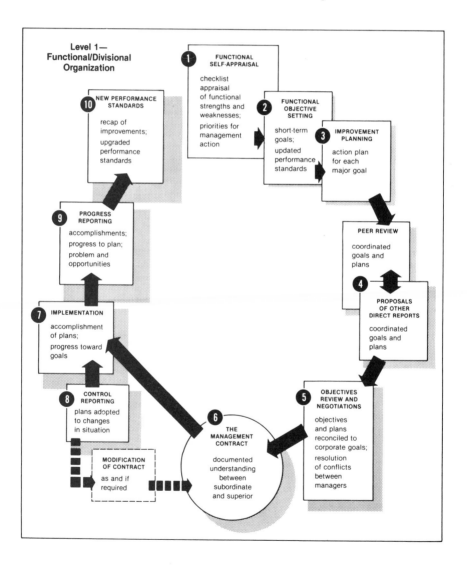

Each of the steps in the process is discussed in depth and detail in the chapters which follow. Because the contract is the most novel element of the process, however—and because it is potentially the most controversial—the next few pages are given to a brief discussion of its nature and role in the total process, together with a description of its format. (This will be enlarged upon later, in its proper chapter sequence as Step 6 of the process.)

THE CONTRACT ELEMENTS

The description that follows refers to the contract between you and your organizational superior. Its principles and mode of operation apply to the contract between you and each of your direct-reporting subordinates.

The actual contract between you and your organizational superior need only be a simple document. Its essential elements are:

- A list of your major objectives for your function
- Your considered plan of action (improvement plan) designed to achieve these goals
- Identification of the resources you need to carry out your plan and the costs of these resources
- Specification of the leadership style you consider appropriate for each major task
- The signatures of both parties

WHAT THESE ELEMENTS REPRESENT

Implicit in these five contract elements is *commitment* on the part of both of you to work together toward accomplishment of objectives that are at once beneficial to the organization and rewarding to yourselves.

- *Your list of objectives* represents your commitment to accomplish a set of defined results by a specific time. Concurrence of your boss with these objectives represents a commitment on his or her part to support your efforts to achieve the specified goals and not to change them for specious or self-serving reasons.
- *The plan* represents your commitment to take specific actions at specified times and to accomplish these tasks within stated time and cost limits. By concurring with your plan, your boss contracts and commits to make no untoward demands upon your time that would prevent these actions from being taken and deadlines met.

concurring with your *identification of resources needed*, your perior contracts to provide whatever additional money, facilities, tools, and people you need to implement your plan. Your acceptance of this agreement represents your commitment to employ these resources productively.

- *Agreement with the leadership style* you have specified implies commitment by your boss to provide the amount and type of guidance, supervision, and instruction that you feel you need to carry out the major tasks of your plan.

- The *signatures* of the two parties represent mutual commitment to honor the terms and spirit of the agreement. This is necessary because even the best of intentions can go awry under the pressure of conflicting demands, unanticipated events, and personal ambitions.

The multipart statement—objectives, action plan, resources required, and leadership style—becomes a *contract* through discussion and negotiation between you and your organizational superior. Your signatures on the document represent a formalizing of the resulting agreement.

The contract itself can take one of several forms, providing that the foregoing essentials are contained in it; one suggested format that has proved useful is given in Figure 5.2.

THE CONTRACT FORMAT—OBJECTIVES
AND IMPROVEMENT MATRIX

The form illustrated in Figure 5.2 is called the Objectives and Improvement Matrix. It is the single mandatory form required by the system, aside from the self-appraisal checklists.

The form itself had its origin in a program developed at the highest level of ITT in the mid-sixties, although it has gone through several mutations since then. Harold Geneen became concerned about the effectiveness of the production functions in the manufacturing divisions and subsidiaries. He communicated his concern to Richard E. Bennett, a staff vice president and possessor of one of the brightest industrial engineering minds in the corporation. (Bennett is now senior executive vice president of ITT, with responsibility for three of the corporation's five worldwide groups.)

Bennett was convinced from his own personal observation that some of the most profitable operating units were making money in spite of themselves—that they were enjoying the benefit of a fast-growing market that masked their internal inefficiencies. (There is some reason to suspect that Bennett planted the concern in Geneen's mind in order to get his chief's support for an improvement program.) How much *more* profitable these units could be, he reasoned, if their operations were really efficient and truly productive.

The two executives' concern was translated into an operations audit program called the ITT Worldwide Plant-Rating Grid, which was implemented in ITT manufacturing units throughout the world under Bennett's direction. (I did the initial development work that led to the final program, including design of the original form on which the ratings were entered.)

The program included some 2 dozen operating functions, covered by a broader conception of industrial engineering than is conventionally used—described by Bennett as "wall-to-wall" coverage. In the early seventies, the program was expanded to encompass a number of marketing and sales functions.

By then I had joined a large telecommunications company, where I adapted the concept and the format to a service operation in a single area of the company. It was found to be quite practicable for service functions. (The program was never implemented companywide, however, because of internal opposition to disturbing the status quo.) The form was subsequently modified and improved for use in a sizable ($600 million sales) building-products company. Here it became part of the AIM Program, an acronym for Appraisal and Improvement Matrix, as the form was then entitled. In this application, the form became more tightly integrated with the checklists used to evaluate each function. At this point, as well, the "total system" implications of the program became apparent to me; the potential of the process for improving managerial productivity became evident; and the concept of management by contract began to take shape.

The Objectives and Improvement Matrix is the only form needed; it is designed to contain *all essential information* about your functional objectives and improvement plans for the coming year. This matrix must be supported by the self-appraisal checklists (described in Chapter 6) as well as some detailed plan support.

This form provides for a close linkage between objectives and the related improvement plans; it also provides a link to the self-appraisal checklists upon which the objectives are based. One section of the form serves as a factual data base against which the information contained in the other sections can be tested for reasonableness.

After approval and acceptance by your organizational superior,

Figure 5.2 THE CONTRACT FORM—OBJECTIVES AND IMPROVEMENT MATRIX

Any Company FE

Objectives and Improvement Matrix
☐ Marketing and Sales
☐ Production Operations

FUNCTION

A. DATA BASE

1. IDENTIFICATION DATA

a. Group:
b. Unit:
c. Location:
d. Product Line:

2. SIZE-UP DATA

3. PERFORMANCE DATA

B. SUMMARY APPRAISAL RATINGS

No.	Topic	Rating
1	General management of the function	
2	Structure and operation of the function	
3	Functional power and responsibility	
4	Measurements and control reports	
5	Operating performance assessment	
6	Front-office support and recognition	
7	Communications and coordination	
8	Functional innovation	
9	Functional improvement program	
10	Functional resources	

RATING KEY

A = Above standard
I = Improvement opportunity
M = Major management action needed

	Date
Prepared by:	Date
Reviewed and approved:	Date
Revised and approved:	Date

C. OBJECTIVES

No.	Description	Due	Mgmt Style

Note: Shown reduced; actual size 11" x 8½"

Figure 5.2 THE CONTRACT FORM (Reverse side)

D. IMPROVEMENT PLANS

All dollars in thousands

Objective no.	Action no.	Description of action planned	Respon- sibility for action	Sched. completion date	Estimated benefits		Estimated costs		
					Current year	Annualized	Capital	Expense	
								Curr. yr.	Ann.

Note: Shown reduced; actual size 11″ x 8½″

the form becomes a contract between you and your boss. In similar fashion, acceptance and approval by you of the matrix forms containing the objectives and improvement plans of your subordinates constitutes a contract between each of them and you.

The form is divided into four sections:

Section A. Data Base

The purpose of the data base is to provide an information backdrop of hard numbers, ratios, and relationships against which your appraisal objectives and improvement plans can be evaluated by your boss. It is in three parts:

Identification data include identification of your function, its organizational relationships in terms of the group and unit of which it is part, its geographic location if necessary, and, if applicable, the product line to which it relates.

Size-up data provide a base of general information on volume of output, size of work force, size of facility, and the like, varying with the function.

Performance data provide information on measurable current functional performance. This may show, for example, the actual number of invoices processed, output per invoice clerk per day or week, average time per processing, and cost per invoice. A comparison with a similar prior period is useful to put current performance into perspective.

This data base section can be set up with columns and lines to suit the unique characteristics of the organization being appraised, if desired.

Section B. Summary Appraisal Ratings

The essential purpose of this section of the matrix is to serve as a link or bridge between your functional self-appraisal (described next in Chapter 6) and the objectives you set for your function (described in Chapter 7).

The ten topics listed are the captions for the ten major subdivisions of the detailed self-appraisal checklists given in the next chapter. Each topic will be given a summary rating derived from the detailed self-appraisal that you make, using the checklists as a guide. It is recommended that these summary ratings be expressed in terms of "A" for *above standard*, "I" for *improvement opportunity*, and "M" for *management action needed.* (These ratings are discussed further at the end of Chapter 6.)

Obviously, your ratings can never be really scientific and are almost sure to be less than completely objective. After all, you are evaluating your own performance to some extent. Honesty, however, is essential if you are serious about improving your own performance. Judgment and intuition are involved, as well as a perfectly natural bias. A measure of self-protection is also a factor. Unquestionably, you will want, and should have, assurance from your boss that the results of your self-appraisal will not be used against you should they be unfavorable.

As your subordinates go through the same self-rating process, they need the same reassurance, or perhaps even more so, being lower on the organizational totem pole. In this connection, your managers should be encouraged to review their initial ratings with the program coordinator before exposing them to you, their supervisor. The coordinator's role is to guide the managers toward more objective, less biased, evaluations.

Obviously, certain of your subordinates will need more guidance and "conditioning" than others, especially during early implementation of the process. In the case of some subordinates, it may be beneficial for you to make an independent checklist appraisal and matrix summary rating, then to discuss (and resolve) any differences in ratings with these individuals before they proceed to develop their objectives and action plans. In any case, there is no "one best way" to implement the program; a tailoring of approaches to the personalities and perceived needs of the various subordinate managers is called for. As managers gain confidence and experience, the need for outside intervention should lessen.

(It must be pointed out that some individuals simply cannot tolerate or adjust to a goals-oriented, results-are-what-count work environment. Nor is it necessary that every single individual do so—the process will produce substantial benefits even though participation is less than 100 percent. Accommodations should be made, however, for those unable to adapt, in order that their individual contributions to the organization will not be lost.)

Sections C and D. Objectives and Improvement Plans

This step in the preparation of the matrix is a two-phase process: first, development of *objectives* that respond to needs exposed by your functional self-appraisal; then development of *improvement plans* spelling out in specific terms the actions that will be taken to achieve each stated goal. Objectives and plans cannot be separated. Together they represent your committed forward contribution to the organization's objectives; together they form the basis for negotiating the management contract with your boss. This is the purpose of Sections C and D of the matrix.

In Section C, "Objectives," you should list an objective, or objectives, for each topic which you rated less than "A" (above standard). Objectives should be keyed to the appraisal topics by number. Then in Section D, you should detail an action plan for each objective, again keyed by number.

An objective that is unsupported by an action plan is indicative of lack of commitment on the part of the manager. Conversely, an action plan not directed specifically to the carrying out of a stated objective is evidence that the manager may have thought in narrow terms of task or activity, rather than goal achievement.

Obviously, an objective that is unrelated and unresponsive to the appraisal ratings and to the answers on the detailed checklists must be questioned. If, despite this, the objective appears to be a valid one, then its source must be determined; if not, then the manager's interpretation of his or her self-appraisal should be reviewed.

Your objectives and action plans should focus on major and critical factors that will contribute most to the overall objectives of the enterprise. No manager, no organization, no business enterprise ever has so much time, talent, and money that resources can be dissipated in the attempt to overcome every deficiency, correct every weakness. Emphasis should be directed toward improving those factors within your function that build and reinforce the organization's strengths in the marketplace, the factors that enhance the company's competitive uniqueness. Every function of the organization, no matter how remote its activities may seem to be from the customer, has an effect on product quality, customer service, price competitiveness, and timely delivery. Your function (and every other) contributes to the unique set of characteristics that distinguishes the successful business from the mediocre.

Your task, therefore, is to identify the factors in your function which, through application of your management intelligence and effort, will strengthen the total company's position vis-à-vis its competition and make it a more viable contender in the company's markets. In this way, you make your personal contribution to the survival and perpetuation of the enterprise. This task is not an easy one, and it cannot be accomplished without a strong and supportive relationship between you and your subordinates, your peers, and your organizational superior. The management by contract program is intended, above all, to help build and sustain these relationships.

(Objective setting is discussed at length in Chapter 7; improvement planning in Chapter 8.)

In the final column of Section C you are requested to indicate the kind of leadership role that you desire your superior to assume for each objective on the list. *The effect of this is to set up your own self-control limits.* In those instances where you are experienced and confident of your ability to accomplish the objective, and you feel that you need few instructions and little supervision from your boss, you may indicate a low task, low relationship style. In other cases, where your experience is limited and your confidence level is relatively low, you may elect to choose a high task, high relationship style, meaning that firm instruction and fairly close supervision from your boss are welcomed. There are degrees of both, of course, which can be negotiated during the dialogue between you and your organizational superior in Step 5 of the process. This is discussed further in Chapter 10.

NOTE

[1] George Odiorne, "The Politics of Implementing MBO," *Business Horizons,* June 1974.

TEN STEPS TO MANAGEMENT BY CONTRACT

Each step in the process is described in terms of its contribution to the productivity of the individual manager as well as to the organization as a whole. Particular emphasis should be given to the three steps through which the individual managers' objectives are successively harmonized with those of other managers and reconciled with the overall goals of the enterprise; these are discussed in Chapters 8, 9, and 10.

PART THREE

HOW TO BUILD A
FOUNDATION OF FACTS

THE FUNCTIONAL SELF-APPRAISAL—
STEP 1 OF THE PROCESS

The crucial first step in the management by contract process—the basis for all subsequent steps—is an evaluation of your function or activity, which you make yourself. This in-depth appraisal is an essential prerequisite to the development of your functional objectives and improvement program. Its primary purpose is to secure your goals and plans to a factual foundation of existing capabilities, current performance standards, and available resources.

This appraisal must be made by you, the functional manager—not by an outside agency. Operations audits conducted by professional auditors are a business essential, of course, but they are not part of *this* process. In order that your objectives and your improvement plans will represent genuine commitment, they must be built upon your own analysis of the situation *as you see it*, not as it is seen and evaluated by someone else. The process provides guidance as well as checks and balances to ensure that your self-appraisal will be thorough and effective.

(A further factor in the decision to make the audit a self-appraisal is that operations audits conducted by professional internal auditors are sometimes perceived by functional managers to be threatening, even punitive. As a consequence many managers tend to be less than candid in their responses to auditors' questionnaires and less than fully cooperative in correcting deficiencies exposed by the audits.)

When this foundation of self-appraisal is lacking, objectives have a tendency to become hopes and desires rather than realistic, achievable goals. The improvement plans developed subsequently may then reflect the impractical character of the objectives by imposing tasks that are beyond people's

**CHAPTER
SIX**

capabilities, by setting deadlines that ignore existing commitments, and by utilizing resources that are out of reach.

In such a case, as time goes on and it becomes apparent that the objectives can't be attained, a manager may begin to look around for an excuse or a scapegoat on which to pin the failure. The first of these can divert a manager's energies into nonproductive channels; the second can create serious counterproductive tensions and conflicts within the organization. In the worst case, a manager may resort to "creative reporting" to cover up the lack of progress—this can compound the problem by further misdirecting human energies and resources toward unattainable ends.

It would be unrealistic in the extreme to expect individuals to conduct critical, penetrating, nonsubjective evaluations of their own functions without a good deal of guidance and assistance—and a degree of assurance that any deficiencies that are exposed by the appraisal will not be used against them. Self-appraisal is not the most comfortable of disciplines. For this reason and because this basic step is so important to the process, managers must be provided with instructions to guide them through the appraisal and with a coach, in the form of a program coordinator, to turn to for assistance. These are essential elements for effective working of the process.

A requirement that may be too obvious to mention is sufficient time free from daily work pressures to develop the self-appraisal. A sound analytical appraisal requires intense concentration. It also takes time—as much as several days in some cases. It must be stressed, however, that this is a good investment of your time, for the whole process begins here.

It is extremely important that your objectives are based upon a self-appraisal that is thorough, searching, and objective. Above all, you must be honest with yourself. Keep in mind always that you are evaluating your function, not your own performance. Admittedly, it is not easy to keep the two separate. To guide you through the self-appraisal, a set of detailed Checklists has been prepared. They cover ten important aspects of functional management, as follows:

1. General management of the function
2. Structure and operation of the function
3. Functional power and responsibility
4. Functional measurements and controls
5. Functional performance assessment
6. Front-office support for the function
7. Communication and coordination with other functions

8. Functional innovation in methods and techniques
9. Functional improvement programs
10. Functional resources

These Checklists will be found in Chapter 20, right after Chapter 19's "Manager's Guide to the Functional Self-Appraisal," designed to "walk you through" the appraisal. (A sample of the Checklist is given later in this chapter, along with specific instructions for its use.)

THE RATIONALE UNDERLYING THE FUNCTIONAL SELF-APPRAISAL

Because the functional self-appraisal is so crucial to the entire process of management by objectives and self-control, it seems necessary and appropriate at this point in the discussion to describe the logic or rationale upon which the appraisal is based. Accordingly, the next several pages are intended to put this important step into its proper perspective as part of the management process.

The Objectives Gap

In many if not most conventional MBO programs, objectives are established at the very highest organizational level for the enterprise as a whole, then fanned outward and downward, in a pattern resembling the organizational hierarchy, to become first the subobjectives for divisions, then for departments, and finally for individual managers. The responsible executives and managers are brought into the process at the various stages; at these points, they are expected to participate in the development of the objectives for their respective areas of operation, within the constraints and the framework of the overall objectives.

When efficiently carried out, this process produces a structure of objectives into which each subobjective neatly fits, like a block of stone in a pyramid. Executives and managers alike are aware of their roles and expected contributions. The pattern is pleasing to the senses and provides great assurance to the top executive that the organization is under tight control. In theory, organizational units whose performance is on track need little or no attention, leaving the CEO free to work with the problem units who, by failing to meet their committed goals, are jeopardizing the attainment of the total corporate objectives.

The process gives the appearance of management by objectives, but the appearance may be deceptive. Virtually every practitioner agrees that the essential ingredient in an effective MBO program is participation in the setting of objectives. In the process described, the manager is not really participating; he or she is merely *endorsing* the objectives of the *higher* organizational unit and is influencing only the objectives of units *lower* in the hierarchy. The manager has little or no involvement with, or influence on, the objectives of other functions or higher organizational levels. The individual's own objectives are shaped not by the manager but by others—they are a direct function of the higher-level goal. If they were otherwise, they would not be accepted.

Often, there can be a serious discontinuity between the overall goals of the organization and the capabilities and resources of an individual function. This can be in either direction: the function may be capable of much higher performance than is demanded of it, or it may be short of the required resources. Almost never is there complete compatibility. In the former case, it is all too easy to accept the objective, knowing that its achievement will cause no strain. In the latter, there is a tendency to accept the objective despite the lack of resources with the hope that somehow a little more effort and some good fortune will overcome the deficiencies.

There can be an even more serious gap between the corporate objectives and the manager's personal development goals. The mating of the two is often a shotgun wedding, and in the process it is the personal goals that are compromised. In either case, the subobjectives are force-fitted into the overall goal. Those who resist are considered nonconformist, and the system tends to either bend the individuals into shape or break them.

Objectives and Commitment

Despite their apparent involvement, many managers operating under this system have an uneasy feeling that the goals they have pledged to achieve have been forced upon them. As a consequence, the goals may lack the full commitment and dedication that is so essential to the achievement of extraordinary objectives.

Management by objectives and self-control is not a simple process, nor is it the most comfortable discipline for managers to follow. The setting of meaningful objectives may well be the most difficult and the most demanding part of the whole process. Yet some programs give this phase of MBO far less attention than it deserves, as though assuming that objective setting were a natural function of person and manager. Decidedly, it is not. Nor is it sufficient to give a manager only the guidance of a larger, broader objective within which to develop lesser goals—a good manager needs much more, and so does the organization.

The needs of the total enterprise are not served by a system which fails to provide the individual manager with the guidance, direction, and assistance needed to develop good objectives. Neither are the organization's needs met by a process which excludes the manager from full and productive involvement in the establishment of its objectives.

A concept of objective setting that resembles a downward cascading of goals from the topmost level of the organization implies a degree of executive wisdom that seldom, if ever, exists. It fails to comprehend inputs of knowledge, information, and insight from operating people that could profoundly improve the shape and direction of the overall objectives. Worse, it rejects important input from the outside world in which the enterprise functions, the real world from which the top executives of the organization are all too often insulated.

Objective setting must begin not at the top but at the bottom of the managerial pyramid. There, objectives must be anchored to a solid base of hard information, not erected upon the shifting sands of speculation, bias, conjecture, and personal opinion. There, too, is where objectives are supported by personal commitment.

This is in no way an argument against the establishment of broad, long-range corporate strategic goals by the executive office. On the contrary, that is a proper and vital function of that level of the organization, along with policy formulation, organizational development, and resource allocation. What is being cautioned against is a rigid, inflexible imposition of objectives upon all levels of management—the kinds of objectives that tend to limit rather than motivate people, to constrain rather than challenge managers.

Need for Functional Self-Appraisal

In order that objectives will be based on a bedrock of "unshakable" facts, objective setting must be preceded by a process of critical self-appraisal. Just as one must be aware of one's personal strengths and weaknesses before meaningful goals for self-improvement can be developed, a functional manager must be aware of the strengths and deficiencies of the function before goals can be developed that will enhance its contribution to the total organization.

The ten-point functional self-appraisal is designed to guide and assist each functional manager in the conduct of this evaluation. The self-appraisal is intended to form a firm, durable, and verifiable foundation of facts coupled with critical analysis and evaluation upon which a set of objectives for each basic function and organizational unit of the company can be built. These objectives are then brought together at successively higher levels and integrated to form the bases for the development of objectives for larger organizational units. At the highest level, the formulation of overall corporate objectives is guided by structured summary inputs from all levels and functions of the organization.

To be effective, the appraisal must follow a definite sequence. It is not enough simply to question whether important tasks are being done properly; the sequential relationship between tasks must be considered. Some tasks can be accomplished only after certain other conditions have been satisfied—to appraise such tasks before having established whether or not the essential preconditions exist would be futile. Obviously, it is pointless to question whether the performance records and operating control reports of the function are adequate, without having first determined that the function has an operating budget covering expenses for recordkeeping and report preparation. Similarly, to appraise the adequacy of the manpower resources of the function before being assured that the functional head has proper authority to hire people, is to put the cart before the horse.

Emphasis on Output

The sequence followed in this appraisal procedure has been carefully selected in this light. Throughout the appraisal, the emphasis is on *output*, not on activity or input. The appraisal is intended to evaluate the effectiveness of the function, not the efficiency of the activities performed by its personnel. The distinction is a critical one—it is the difference between results and efforts. It is possible to perform a task efficiently without achieving a beneficial result; that is, one can be extremely efficient without being the least bit effective. Cases in point, not uncommon in the corporate world, are the development of a very efficient computerized management-control system that either is never implemented or falls into disuse because the operating people were not sold on its benefits to them, or the superbly written business plan that is never implemented because line managers were not involved in its preparation.

The self-appraisal recognizes that every function is concerned with input, activity, and output.

$$\text{INPUT} \xrightarrow{\text{plus}} \text{ACTIVITY} \xrightarrow{\text{equals}} \text{OUTPUT}$$

Managers can become so involved with either input or activity that they lose sight of their real purpose, which is output; two such types are the "overcontroller" who believes that saving money and husbanding resources is the prime purpose of business, and the compulsive "doer" who measures worth to the organization by long hours put in at a desk, number of meetings held, and size of staff.

The appraisal is concerned with activity, of course, but only to the extent that it is related to the mission, or charter, of the function. Whether or not individuals are performing their assigned tasks properly is the supervisory side of a personnel problem and not a concern of the appraisal.

Input is a concern of the appraisal to the extent that it is a major determinant of the quality and quantity of the output, hence the productivity, of the function. Discussions on industrial or clerical productivity improvement tend to focus on the process—on the activity—as though the quality of input were a given. To assume so is to overlook opportunities to increase productivity by improving the quality of the initial input. A rather common situation is a customer-order processing system whose output may be improved significantly by redesigning the sales order form filled out by the field salesperson. Because the order form is the *input* to the processing group at the home office, processing time frequently can be reduced and accuracy improved with little or no additional effort on the part of the salesperson.

Industry has found that it is clearly more productive to assure that the input to the process meets predetermined standards of quality, rather than to process substandard input in the hope that the imperfect product will be rejected after processing. It follows that control during the process assures that each successive step in the sequence is performed properly, because the output of each step provides the input to the next. In this sense, quality assurance is control of *inputs*, not outputs.

Contribution to Competitive Effectiveness

The self-appraisal is vitally concerned with the capabilities of the function to contribute to the total competitive effectiveness of the enterprise in the marketplace. These capabilities are, in the final analysis, the raison d'être of every function, regardless of how remote the function may appear to be from the ultimate user of the company's products.

As an example, the effectiveness of plant maintenance, a function not ordinarily thought of in terms of the marketplace, should be determined by *its contribution to the output of goods and services that meet the quality and cost standards demanded by the marketplace.* To this end, the ability of the function to keep all equipment producing good products efficiently and to keep all facilities in good repair without incurring excessive costs is really a measure of its competitive effectiveness.

It is critically important to focus the attention of individual functional managers on the marketplace and to force them to think in terms of the effect of every action upon the customer and the user of the product. Failure to do so can lead to organizations so concerned with improving their internal efficiency, and managers so engrossed in enhancing their professional competency, that the real objectives of the enterprise may be overlooked.

Another concern of the appraisal is the ability of functional management to plan, organize, delegate, and control tasks—an ability that is derived from adequate authority, an effective internal organization, documented procedures, and a good control system. The appraisal is designed to regard each function not simply as an organizational unit but *as a management process, a system of organized activities* by means of which people work together to achieve a desired result.

Finally, the self-appraisal seeks to identify and isolate for management attention those aspects of the function most critical to progress toward overall company objectives.

Functional Appraisal and Job Understanding

Self-appraisal is not an easy task, nor is it usually made without causing some measure of discomfort, often chagrin, to the manager. The analysis often exposes areas of management weakness in organization, control reporting, operating methods, or coordination with other functions. It should be emphasized, however, that the appraisal is being made of the *function*, not of the individual manager. Assurance must be given that the deficiencies that managers disclose will not be used against them.

Typically, the appraisal results in a lengthy list of deficiencies, weaknesses, and problems—sometimes to the extent that the manager may despair of ever overcoming them all. At this point, the manager's task is to identify the factors that will contribute most to the overall company and its total competitive effectiveness. Application of the well-known 80/20 rule will reduce the list to the critical few items that make the difference and weed out the trivial many items that haven't much effect on the overall results. This is an essential step in the process, if the subsequent list of functional objectives is to be a manageable one.

The first result of the functional self-appraisal is a better understanding of the manager's job, in terms of results expected and the individual tasks that constitute the function. Functional results don't just happen; they come only from tasks being accomplished by people. Tasks are accomplished only when individuals work at them in a purposeful way, alone or in organized groups. Basic to this is resolution of the uncertainties that surround every task—why it must be done, what is to be done, when it must be completed, how it should be performed, and who is to do it.

These uncertainties are resolved only when:

- The purpose of the task is clearly defined.
- The nature of the task is specified precisely.
- A time schedule for completion is established.
- Procedures and standards are documented.
- The task is assigned to an individual.

The appraisal identifies for the manager tasks that may be unassigned or whose assignment is unclear, tasks that are being duplicated to some extent, tasks that are not clearly defined in terms of purpose or nature, and tasks lacking procedures or standards of performance. Normally, most of these tasks will be within the manager's own function, although some may be the responsibility of people in other functions. Tasks that are the manager's responsibility should be documented on updated job descriptions (discussed later).

HOW TO USE THE
SELF-APPRAISAL CHECKLISTS

The Checklists are intended to guide you through your functional self-appraisal with the least expenditure of time. They are structured in a way that allows you to give your full attention to the *content* of your appraisal by eliminating any need for you to concern yourself with *format*.

Each point on the Checklist is stated in the form of a positive statement that expresses an ideal condition for which you should strive. As an example, one point states: "Actual cost savings are compared with target amounts and percentages at least every quarter." You are expected to respond "yes" if the statement is generally true of the function; "no" if you consider the statement not to be true, and "sometimes or partially" if the statement is less than completely true. In the event that the statement may not apply to a particular situation, "not applicable" is written in the space for response. In other cases where data may be lacking on which to base a definitive reply, "not answerable" is written in. You are appraising your own function, of course, so you can hardly be expected to be totally objective and unbiased—however, it should be emphasized that you are reviewing your *function*, not your own performance.

It goes without saying that negative responses to the Checklists indicate problems within the function and that the greater their number the more serious the situation. But there also can be too many "yes" answers; this may indicate that the reviewer is not sufficiently critical or objective. A great many less than positive responses ("sometimes or partially") can point to internal weaknesses and lack of firm direction. A lot of "not applicable" responses may indicate that the reviewer is avoiding the issues. More than a few "not answerable" responses is symptomatic of inadequate records or obsolete data bases.

You will find, as you proceed with your functional self-appraisal, that the points covered by the Checklists relate to generic management factors, not to the technical aspects of the function itself. That is to say, for example, that if you are a plant maintenance manager, the self-appraisal does not seek to determine whether or not you maintain a 96 percent machine up-time record in the fabrication department or whether you keep departmental overtime to below 5 percent. These are, of course, vitally important factors, but they are not the purpose of this appraisal.

What these Checklists are intended to provide is *assurance* to you, the functional manager, that your function is structured and administered in a manner that promotes innovation and high productivity; that it possesses the power, status, visibility, and recognition it needs to get support from other functions and from topside; and that its relationships with other functions are constructive and harmonious rather than adversary and obstructive. The Checklists seek further to assure you that your function is concerned with *output* and *results* rather than mere busyness and that your function expects high standards of performance from all its people, not just for the company's sake but for their own self-esteem and development as individuals. Finally, their purpose is to determine whether your function is provided with the resources needed to carry out its mission effectively and meet its objectives.

The professional and operating aspects of most functions are covered by the many technical and professional handbooks and reference manuals currently available.

HOW TO SCORE AND RATE
YOUR SELF-APPRAISAL

Each section of the self-appraisal Checklist is followed by a suggested scoring and rating system designed to tell the reviewer whether the condition and performance of the function are satisfactory or not and then to give the reviewer an indication of its degree of satisfaction. The rating system is simple. Each item on the Checklist to which the answer is "yes" is given *one full point*. Each to which the response is "sometimes or partially" is given *one-half point*. Each item answered "no" is scored *zero*. The total number of points scored is divided by the total number of items on the list and multiplied by 100 to arrive at the rating percentage. In most cases, a rating of less than 65 percent is unacceptable and calls for an improvement program. Obviously, the lower the rating, the more drastic the action required becomes.

EXAMPLE:

Guidance of Policies/Objectives/Strategies

	Yes	No	S/P*
Changes in policy are communicated promptly to appropriate personnel and are explained.	✓		
Recommendations for policy changes are sent up for executive consideration.	✓		
Corporate objectives are communicated to functional personnel to the extent appropriate for effective job performance.			✓
Corporate strategies and plans are communicated to functional personnel to the extent consistent with company security.	✓		
Functional objectives are known to all personnel.		✓	
Each person's required contribution to these goals is known and accepted as a personal goal.		✓	
TOTAL POINTS	3	+0+	.5	= 3.5

RATING:

$$\frac{\text{Enter number of points scored} \quad \boxed{3.5}}{\text{Enter number of items on checklist} \quad \boxed{6}} = \boxed{.58} \times 100 = \boxed{58\%}$$

Admittedly, this suggested method for scoring and grading the self-appraisal is unsophisticated, even elementary. It obviously lacks a weighting system designed to give higher values to certain points on

* Sometimes or Partially

the Checklist that may be more important than others. What is critical to one organization, however, may be irrelevant to another, so it would be inappropriate, if not presumptuous, for someone outside the organization to assign different values to individual topics. If weighting is considered necessary, the rating system may be revised to suit the characteristics and needs of your function and the organization.

SELF-APPRAISAL CHECKLISTS

(This is a sample of the Checklists. The complete set is in Chapter 20.)

1. GENERAL MANAGEMENT OF THE FUNCTION

A. Business Mission

	Yes	No	S/P*
(1) The function operates under a well-defined business mission or statement of purpose that delineates the scope of its activities and guides and governs its relationships with others.	___	___	___
(2) The mission is in writing, not simply in the mind of its manager.	___	___	___
(3) The mission is published in a document that is available to:			
■ Functional personnel	___	___	___
■ Personnel of other functions having a need to know	___	___	___
(4) The mission has been reviewed *and revised* during the past 12 months.	___	___	___

B. Guidance of Policies/Objectives/Strategies

(1) Corporate policies are made available to all functional personnel having a need for such guidance.	___	___	___
(2) Policies are known and understood by those whose actions they govern.	___	___	___

* Sometimes or Partially

(3) Functional personnel have been informed through meetings and individual discussions about their obligations and responsibilities to these policies. — — —

(4) Changes in policy are communicated promptly to appropriate personnel and are explained. — — —

(5) Recommendations for policy changes are sent up for executive consideration. — — —

(6) Corporate objectives are communicated to functional personnel to the extent appropriate for effective job performance. — — —

(7) Corporate strategies and plans are communicated to functional personnel to the extent consistent with company security. — — —

(8) Functional objectives are known to all personnel. — — —

(9) Each person's required contribution to these goals is known and accepted as a personal goal. — — —

(10) All such personnel have been advised that strategies are "company confidential" information. — — —

C. Performance Standards

(1) Standards have been set for the performance of all major functional tasks. — — —

(2) These performance standards are documented in job descriptions, and are available to affected personnel. — — —

(3) All functional people know that their performance is being measured and compared to high standards. — — —

(4) Standards are reviewed regularly and revised periodically. — — —

(5) Actual performance is recorded and compared to standards frequently. — — —

(6) Productivity improvement goals have been set for all definable tasks. — — —

(7) Actual productivity improvement is compared with goals at least quarterly. — — —

(8) Cost reduction targets in dollars and percent have been established for each subfunction. — — —

(9) Actual cost savings are compared to target amounts and percentages at least every quarter. — — —

(10) Quality standards have been set for all outputs
of the function.

(11) The actual quality of output is measured and
compared with standards quarterly.

TOTAL POINTS $\boxed{}$ $+0+$ $\boxed{}$ $= \boxed{}$

RATING:

$$\frac{\text{Enter number of points scored } \boxed{}}{\text{Enter number of items on Checklist } \boxed{}} = \boxed{} \times 100 = \boxed{} \%$$

SETTING PRIORITIES FOR OBJECTIVES

It was noted in an earlier chapter that self-appraisal is not an easy or a comfortable task. It is not unusual for the Checklist appraisal to result in a long list of deficiencies—perhaps to the degree that you might wonder whether and how you can ever correct them all. *Be advised that you cannot and you should not.*

Your task at this point is to set priorities. This is a three-step process of (1) analyzing your Checklist appraisal, (2) applying Pareto's rule to isolate the "critical few factors that make the difference" from the "trivial many," and (3) translating your self-appraisal into a summary rating. Pareto's rule, you will recall, says that in most situations about 20 percent of the factors account for 80 percent of the results. In a typical inventory situation, for example, some 20 percent of the items in stock account for approximately 80 percent of the total inventory value, and in a typical product distribution situation 15 to 20 percent of the dealers sell 80 to 85 percent of the volume. When you control the 20 percent, you have effective control of the situation—at far less cost than attempting to control 100 percent.

The critical factors on your Checklist appraisal are the ones for which you will set objectives—the others will be controlled through performance standards contained in job descriptions. The "bridge" from the Checklists to your objectives list is Section B of the matrix described earlier in Chapter 5. It is here that you should apply a summary rating to each of the ten major topics in your self-appraisal. It is suggested that your ratings be expressed in these terms:

A = Above Standard—in cases where most of your responses to the detailed Checklist are in the "yes" column and the score is high

I = Improvement Opportunity—in cases where your responses indicate that management action will be beneficial to your function and to the overall operation

M = Management Action Needed—in cases where many of your responses are in the "no" column and the score is low or where certain of the more critical items are clearly deficient in your judgment

Normally, an objective and improvement plan should be developed for each topic given a summary rating of "M." Some topics rated "I" may also call for an objective. A high degree of management judgment and selectivity is required. (Objective setting is discussed in depth in Chapter 7.)

HOW TO CREATE
YOUR OWN CHALLENGE

FUNCTIONAL OBJECTIVE SETTING—
STEP 2 OF THE PROCESS

The second major step in the process is determining the principal objectives that your function will work toward during the next 12 months. Development of these goals requires three inputs: (1) the preceding in-depth appraisal of your functional strengths and weaknesses, (2) an evaluation of your current functional resources, capabilities, and performance standards, and (3) knowledge of the company's objectives, strategies, policies, plans, programs, and standards—sufficient, at least, to give you an understanding of the direction the firm is heading in.

Having pared down your list of functional tasks to the critical few, you are now in a position to concentrate your management skills on the improvement of these factors. At this point, your attention should be focused on functional *strengths* rather than on weaknesses or deficiencies. By strengths is meant those aspects of your function that contribute most to the company's capabilities to compete effectively in the marketplace.

There is a natural and inherent tendency for professional managers, whatever their functional discipline, to concentrate on the actions that will enhance their professionalism. As an example, advertising managers are often concerned with enhancing their professional status by winning awards for their advertisements or commercials. While it can be argued that these awards are a tribute to the excellence of the advertising art and copy, they are not its primary purpose. If, in the course of striving for this kind of recognition, managers create advertising that fails to produce inquiries, requests for quotations, and orders for the firm's products, they are not fulfilling their management responsibilities.

It is not the intention to single out advertising managers as a target for

CHAPTER SEVEN

criticism—the same logic applies to every function of the business, no matter how remote it may seem from the marketplace and the user of the product or service.

Also to be avoided is the temptation to concentrate efforts on the correction of every functional weakness. Carried to extremes, this can dissipate management time and scarce resources in a vain striving for perfection in all things. Too often this results in mediocrity in most things.

CONCENTRATION ON CRITICAL GOALS

Your objectives should be listed in Section C of the matrix described in Chapter 5.

It will be noted that the space provided on this form for listing objectives is quite limited. This is an intentional feature of the design; its purpose is to restrict the number of goals that you undertake to accomplish. It was recommended earlier that you should concentrate on objectives that are truly essential to the function and to the total organization. This implies that your goals be few in number rather than many—that your emphasis be on *doing the right something* rather than simply doing many things right. Most managers tend to take on too much, to commit to an excessive number of goals. This can lead to confusion of purpose, dissipation of critical resources, and reduced productivity.

Experience of progressive companies in objective setting has led to a couple of rules of thumb to guide you. The number of objectives should be limited to no more than five or six and you should allocate about 80 percent of your time and resources to these. When the number of objectives exceeds this number, efforts tend to become dissipated and unfocused, to the detriment of your productivity. (It is paradoxical that as your position and rank rise in the organization, the number of objectives you have tends to lessen and they tend to be of more lasting duration.) For there is no more powerful tool to improve productivity than concentration on the tasks that are critical to the enterprise. Conceivably, there can be fewer than five of these, as few as one or two in some cases. Sad experience tells us that if these crucial tasks are left undone or are done inadequately, nothing else that is done seems to matter very much. If, on the other hand, the really compelling goals are met, the other things seem to follow. It is highly probable that if Chrysler had heeded the signals sent by the Arab oil producers in 1974 and had adopted as a single overriding objective the design and production of fuel-efficient vehicles, the company would not have found itself in such deep trouble in the early 1980s.

Certain other principles of objective setting and management by objectives have developed over the years and have been found to be effective in practice. Basic to management by objectives and self-control, it is agreed, is the ability of managers involved to define and articulate objectives that are at once beyond today's reach yet realistic and achievable. These criteria appear to be a contradiction in terms; nevertheless, each is essential and all are interdependent. In addition to these key criteria, objectives should be:

- Clear, positive, and stated in writing
- Based on clear and logical assumptions
- Operational, consistent with other goals, and relevant to the strategy they support
- Controllable by the person responsible
- Specific and measurable
- Directed toward a desired end result

Above all, it must be recognized that the objectives established at the outset of a program or project or those set at the beginning of the operating year *are prime determinants of success or failure.*

It is possible that more projects and programs have failed from lack of proper objectives than from incompetence and inadequate resources. Good objectives are tolerant and forgiving—they allow mistakes in execution. Good objectives are animating and energizing. William James once said that humans tend to live within self-imposed limitations—good objectives can often break down these internalized barriers to achievement. Ordinary people, motivated by exceptional goals, can accomplish extraordinary tasks; but if they are misdirected by inappropriate objectives, the best efforts of capable and well-intentioned people can end in failure of the mission.

Good objectives have a rather magnetic power to attract and capture the resources—the capabilities, funding, and facilities— needed for their achievement. In this connection, a statement of a former secretary-general of the United Nations, U Thant, seems appropriate to paraphrase: "It is no longer resources that limit objectives. Now it can be objectives that create resources . . . perhaps the most revolutionary change man has known."

It follows from this that a large expenditure of management time devoted to establishing high-caliber objectives is time well spent. The first in a list of tasks on any program must be to establish the objectives of the program. Until this is accomplished, *almost nothing else should be done*, because every subsequent action should be derived from and related to the first.

This applies with special emphasis to projects that break new ground—new-product developments and new-market ventures. The essential characteristic of a development project is its future-orientation. There are no "maintenance" functions in a program that is breaking new ground, as there normally are in a mature, fully developed business. Every activity has to be evaluated in terms of progress and must be measured by the distance covered from the starting point to the desired destination—not simply in terms of worker-hours of effort, dollars expended, or size of staff added.

PARETO'S LAW OF OBJECTIVES

One of the major problems that has prevented management by objectives from realizing its promise is the failure of many programs to establish and agree on the goals that are truly critical to the activity and to the total organization. It is absolutely essential to focus attention on *priority* tasks, *critical* tasks; the emphasis must be on "doing the right something," as distinct from the many how-to-do-it programs that are directed toward "doing something right."

Most professional managers are capable of bringing a high order of skill to their assigned jobs. What many lack is an organized method to cope with the multitude of demands and pressures from inside and outside their specialized functions, demands that often translate into activities that tend to divert and dissipate their efforts and energies from the primary mission of the function. What manager, for instance, has not been overwhelmed by the long list of tasks facing him or her and pondered which one should be done first, which second, and which should not be done at all? What manager has not experienced the futility of doing a superb job on a task that should never have been undertaken or should have been abandoned early?

Pareto's famous law of distribution demonstrates that 80 percent of a problem can be attributed to about 20 percent of its variables, that 80 percent of any result is accomplished by about 20 percent of its participants, and that, generally, some 80 to 90 percent of the profits are generated by a small percentage of the products in the line. It is the law that says that in any multivariable situation, a "critical few" factors make most of the difference, while the "trivial many" don't have a significant effect on the total result. The overriding need is to help the manager to cull the list of tasks down to Pareto's critical few. The energies, intelligence, and efforts of the manager can then be concentrated on those tasks that "make the difference."

Identifying the right things to do can be the key to successful management. Objectives will be fewer, more purposeful, and more manageable in terms of measuring actual performance. Too many goals can cause confusion of purpose and diffusion of commitment in much the same way as span of control that is too broad can weaken organization.

Goals and objectives lacking a solid foundation of facts, self-appraisal, and analysis tend to be insubstantial. Goals based on symptoms rather than on intelligent analysis of underlying problems only serve to make problems worse through neglect of root causes. Equally dangerous are those high-minded "global" objectives which seek to exploit promising market opportunities but fail to consider the company's current strengths, resources, and commitments. What company has not been led down the garden path toward promising opportunities for which it lacked the "critical success factors"?

THE DUALITY OF OBJECTIVES

Progress toward achievement of objectives is seldom a smooth process of uninterrupted forward and upward movement. Progress of a project or program, of a business enterprise, of a society, or of an individual is episodic in nature and made in steps and stages— periods of movement followed by periods of consolidation of gains. A program of management by objectives and self-control, to be effective, must take both periods of movement and periods of consolidation into account, because both elements are present in every function at any given time.

It is somewhat analagous to the progress of mountain climbers, who pause periodically to gain strength for the assault on a new height. Their principal concern during each pause is to anchor themselves so as to prevent slipping back—to protect their hard-won gains. Similarly, the managers in a business operation must take preventive action to protect against adverse change by setting stand-ards of performance and controls that will serve as anchors against loss of earlier gains in effectiveness. As an example, the production department, having raised output to 100 widgets per hour through application of good methods engineering, will operate to a standard of 100 pieces per hour until such time as the industrial engineers, together with purchasing, product engineering, quality assurance, and others, have developed ways to increase output to 120 pieces per hour. Thereupon a new standard is adopted while the improvement process is repeated. Initially, of course, an output of 135 pieces per hour may have been adopted as the objective, but it would be unrealistic not to introduce interim improvements into the production process as they become practical and instead wait until all improvements in materials, design, and process had been finalized. Waiting for perfection can be costly.

Management by objectives, in this sense, is a two-stage process. First, standards must be set and results measured by these standards, budgets, or norms. This is the maintenance or consolidation role of management—what Peter Hives calls the "prevention of adverse change." Second, improvement must be achieved through a process of planning and action. This is the creative role of management, "the creation of advantageous change," in Hives's words. The objectives sought are achievement of new, higher standards of performance by a specified point in time. The new standards are then used to measure performance for a period while the next improvement process goes on. (Tosi, Rizzo, and Carroll make a distinction between recurring *routine* and *creative* goals, and suggest that they should be evaluated quite differently—that failure to meet a particularly difficult creative objective should not be judged in the same terms as failure to maintain a critical recurring operation.[1])

The preventive or maintenance function normally is performed by individual persons or departments as a daily routine. An example is customer communications, a subfunction of customer service. If it is assumed that this is a critical area and one in need of management attention (as it surely is in most business organizations), an initial standard might be set as follows: "Customer inquiries and correspondence are answered or acknowledged within 48 hours of receipt."

Obviously, a standard is useful only if we have a way of measuring actual performance and controlling it; that is, identifying substandard performance for corrective action. Without control, a standard is meaningless. In this instance, we require that all customer correspondence and inquiries must be logged in upon receipt and that a record be kept of elapsed time between receipt and response. This can become an expensive and wasteful "paper exercise" unless the manager reviews this report regularly for late responses and seeks to correct the deviations from standard through discipline. It is even more effective to analyze the report for patterns of behavior that can be corrected by taking some predetermined action, such as scheduling overtime work or adding temporary staff until performance is back within standard. "Min-max" control charts are very useful for this task. In any event, maintenance of the standard is a routine objective of the responsible department.

The process of improvement, of creating advantageous change, involves first the setting of a new objective—say, for example, to *acknowledge all inquiries* within 24 hours of receipt and to *answer 90 percent of all inquiries* within 72 hours. Assuming this to be a realistic objective, achievement will require the concerted and coordinated actions of several functions or departments. Among these are the mail room, which must assure that customer correspondence is not delayed once received; the customer-service individual or group who must send out acknowledgments (which very likely vary with the type of inquiry); and the several departments involved in providing help in preparing a specific reply to the customer (these could include production control, engineering, quality assurance, legal, marketing, and others). Everyone must accept the new objective as theirs, everyone must take action to achieve it, and everyone must share accountability for results.

Clearly, this is the phase of management by objectives and self-control that moves the enterprise forward. Measuring and controlling progress toward objectives in this kind of project-oriented management is a different and more complex matter than the process-oriented management discussed earlier. It starts with the need for new organizational forms. The traditional pyramid hierarchy usually employed to control functional performance—for preventive management—is clearly archaic and unworkable for managing change (as it is increasingly recognized to be for managing even routine functions by many progressive companies, but that's another story).

TEAM APPROACH TO OBJECTIVE SETTING

Douglas S. Sherwin, in a recent article entitled "Management of Objectives," describes new organizational forms needed to implement this kind of management. He calls them "objectives teams." His teams are composed of representatives from all functions who can contribute to a particular improvement project. He makes a strong case for making *all* members of each team responsible for results. This is not to imply that the teams are leaderless; a strong team leader is still needed, but the participating members share accountability with the leader and with each other. It is important to distinguish Sherwin's objectives team from the better known and widely used "task force" or project-group approach, which creates organizations separate from the functional one and connected to it only through its leader. He states: "The objectives team rejects the idea of separate organizations—one for change and one for operations—but creates a single organization with both missions to operate the organization and to bring about changes that are established as organization objectives."[2]

This is accomplished by means of an "objectives grid" which is superimposed upon the functional organization to make clear the contribution to change needed from each member of the organization.

Realistically, organizational changes alone will not resolve the inherent tensions and conflicts among people who may be pursuing different goals. Perhaps the most difficult of these to deal with are the natural tensions between people committed to completing a project—the activists—and those committed to protecting and allocating the resources of the company, the "conservatists." Sherwin's objectives teams have the potential to bring these differences out into the open where they may be converted, through discussion, into productive forces.

THE POWER OF POSITIVE OBJECTIVES

The power of positive goals and objectives to animate, energize, and direct the efforts of people and organizations to accomplish remarkable results has been repeatedly demonstrated. The thrill that every American experienced on July 20, 1969, when the first man walked on the surface of the moon, had its source in the objective articulated by President John F. Kennedy 8 years earlier, that within a decade, "We shall land a man on the moon and return him safely to earth."

There is little doubt that this expressed goal energized and motivated the people involved and kept the program moving forward despite adversities and setbacks, even tragedy. Behind every great achievement will be found a similar statement of purpose and intent.

On a lesser plane, major advances in health care, electronics, and communications are reported almost daily. Few of these accomplishments are happenstance; virtually all are the result of good planning, good management, and clear, forceful expressions of objectives.

Most manuals on MBO recommend that the process start with the establishment of objectives for the total corporation or total organization, then fan these out into goals for organizational units. These goals are then subdivided into departmental goals, section goals, and functional goals until the pyramid is complete from apex to base. The task would be simpler if it really worked that way, but it seldom does. ITT's celebrated business planning system under Harold Geneen was very effective for years before his total corporate objectives were clearly articulated and disseminated throughout the organization; it was through the planning process itself, in fact, that quantitative objectives were shaped.

THE ITT EXPERIENCE

It may be more important that the *qualitative* goals of the organization be known and understood. The qualitative factors have been defined as those that pertain to the kind of firm that the managers believe they are running, the choice of markets to be served and how, and the attitudes to be nurtured toward the firm's various publics—in short, the factors which add up to the "character of the firm."

There may have been an unfortunate overpreoccupation with numbers in planning and MBO. Some planners appear to believe that you can't plan what you can't quantify; this apparently follows from the notion that if you can't count it, you can't measure and control it. Putting the controller in charge of business planning, as some have prescribed, can only intensify this trend to the exclusion of the qualitative aspects of business management. The qualitative factors of business mission, company image, company policies, and management style should be planned and measured and monitored just as actively and almost as precisely as the so-called tangibles of business: inventories, accounts receivable, revenues, net income, and cash flow.

To a large degree, the qualitative factors control the quantitative ones. One of Harold Geneen's early actions after taking the reins of ITT in 1959 was to analyze the composition of total revenues and profit in terms of domestic versus international, defense versus commercial, and products versus services. He then articulated a long-range objective for the corporation to achieve a more balanced business mix (as protection against a downturn in any one sector), to lessen reliance on a volatile military market, and to assure shareholders that their dividends were covered by earnings in U.S. dollars.

ITT's is almost a classic case of altering the *quality* of revenues and earnings through planning and MBO. It may well be argued that the long-term goals and objectives implicit in the qualitative statements had to be quantified for measurement and control into percentage shares of domestic revenues versus foreign, commercial versus defense, and services versus products. Nonetheless, the qualitative goals first had to be articulated, understood, and accepted as a precondition to performing the arithmetic.

Similarly, Geneen established objectives for management style.

This is sometimes described as management philosophy; however, the term "style" may be a more fitting term to describe Harold Geneen's forceful and brilliant management. Although these goals probably were not expressed at the time as clearly as they can be seen in retrospect, it is clear that they were firmly set. At the time of his selection as chief executive officer, the style of ITT's management could be characterized as conservative in outlook, passive in response to events, protective of position, inward-looking, and product- and technology-oriented. Geneen's obvious near-term to medium-term objective was to shift the company's style to one of assertive risk-taking after thorough evaluation of all information that could reasonably be made available. Long-range, it was clearly to become market-directed throughout the world and managed by facts, knowledge, and information, with growth to be achieved through leadership in markets, costs, and technology.

ITT's company image badly needed an overhaul in 1959. Surveys indicated that many influential people perceived ITT to be part of AT&T, although it never had been. That elusive quality, image, had to be analyzed in terms of the perception in the minds of the various publics of the company: investors, lenders, employees, customers, competitors, the media, suppliers, the business community, and the general public. The image and style of ITT continued to change and improve (with a couple of notorious lapses) as the corporation grew from a $750 million holding company to a multinational giant generating over $18 billion in sales and revenues. Hardly anyone confuses ITT with AT&T anymore, and not simply because the ampersand was dropped from its logo.

OBJECTIVES-CENTERED COMMAND

In his stimulating book, The Dynamics of Management Control Systems, Arthur E. Mills analyzes control systems in terms of the factors determining values and norms of human behavior and the sources of psychological security to members of an organization.[3] He classifies three sources: the person, the rule, and the task. Each of these gives rise to a style of command: the associated styles of command we call "boss-centered," "rule-centered," and "task-centered." The first two styles of command are found in the majority of organizations, whether business, government, or social. This factor, more than any other, may account for the low state of effectiveness of most government entities and business enterprises. The third style, task-centered management, is far less common; it is more effective but only marginally so.

There is a fourth source of psychological security— achievement— which also gives rise to an associated style of command: "objectives-centered" command. Clearly, this style is not for everyone, but for a great many managers (possibly the majority) it is a style that can promote superior job performance, greater personal gratification, and a high degree of self-actualization.

James L. Hayes, president of American Management Associations, perhaps has said it best: "People dislike work, but they love achievement—the difference is an objective."

Objectives-centered management cannot be arbitrarily imposed upon an organization. There are many managers who are not psychologically receptive to an entrepreneurial "results are what count" style of operation, who cannot function without firm and constant direction, such as the reactive type who responds only to orders and the "bureaupath" who functions by established regulations and rules of order. The system has to accommodate these people and furnish the psychological security they want and need; to force upon them a style of command they cannot tolerate may create within the organization dangerous emotional tensions that can jeopardize the system and reduce its overall effectiveness.

Indeed, the imposition of a new style of management on an existing organization can have traumatic effects upon managers, even those who are psychologically attuned to change. To require managers suddenly "to conceptualize their jobs in terms of ends or objectives rather than activities or means," in the words of Babcock and Sorensen, is not a task to be taken lightly. It is important, therefore, to assess the capability of the organization to assimilate radical change and to modulate the timing of its introduction so as to minimize organizational stresses and "future shock."

Shuster and Kindall, in a 1974 survey of MBO as practiced in Fortune 500 companies, noted that few MBO systems had accomplished what was expected of them.[4] They observed that it may take 5 years before managers are comfortable using the MBO approach.

Babcock and Sorensen also make a strong case for phasing in and implementing MBO over a prolonged period, in order to give managers time to adjust and adapt to what is often a radically new style of operation and a new organizational environment. They say:

> A major change effort such as MBO causes significant organizational "disruption." Indeed, the question of whether or not the strengths of MBO are worth the "cost of jolting the organization with massive and simultaneous changes" is a point well taken. MBO is an additional activity superimposed on employees' existing activities and may well add to the problems of organization dislocation.[5]

They advise that implementation of MBO be staged over a period from 2½ to 7 years in order to "heighten prospects for effective and lasting benefits ₁ . . and enhance opportunities for a final, secure linking with longer-term goals and strategic planning."[6] It is only in their "Stage IV" that integration with other management activities is achieved. Their concern with integration is one that is shared by Heinz Weihrich, who has evaluated the effectiveness of MBO programs by their degree of integration with the key managerial activities of planning, organizing, staffing, directing, and controlling.[7] Weihrich points out that the degree of integration may vary with the organizational environment, the nature of the task, and the organizational level of the participants. It is apparent from these and other studies that integration of MBO with other management functions is essential; Babcock and Sorensen make it clear that such integration cannot be forced, that it comes only with time and a long-range plan of implementation. Both conclusions have important implications to an organization planning to go the MBO route.

LINE AND STAFF OBJECTIVES

The tendency of organization-chart makers to show corporate staffs higher in the echelon and closer to the chief executive has created an unfortunate mind set in staff managers that they exist for a different purpose than line managers. Harold Geneen of ITT spent more than 20 years in the effort to break down the distinction between line and staff. In an early memorandum to his principal staff heads, he expressed the view that staff organizations must be measured in the same terms as the line—that staff effectiveness should be expressed in terms of results only—and that their goals should be the same.

The monthly "staff-effectiveness reports" that resulted from this 1961 directive represented a significant breaking down of the line/staff communication barriers. It forced staff managers to seek out and learn what the line objectives were, and it forced line managers to clarify and articulate these objectives if they were unclear or nonexistent. Then it demanded that staff managers frame their own goals in terms of positive, direct, hands-on support of the line.

Thus it happened that when a division general manager expressed an objective to bring to the market in 2 years a new solid-state telephone PABX and his plan to develop the new product required an upgrading of his engineering staff from electromechanical design skills to electronics, one important objective of the personnel manager became the task of retraining and recruiting the needed capabilities. In other instances, a line manager's goals might be to support a staff objective. A factory manager, for example, may have to set an objective to meet an affirmative action plan goal, developed by Personnel, of hiring more minority employees.

Not all objectives need be sequential, as in these examples. Each manager's self-appraisal of his or her function will reveal internal areas of deficiency that are related to other operations only indirectly, such as the aforementioned personnel manager's need for a computerized employee-capabilities data bank to speed up the search for internal candidates to fill vacancies. In all cases, however, the objectives of both line and staff managers must relate to, support, and reinforce the primary strategic goals of the total organization—these can be expressed either in terms of line or staff operations.

DOCUMENTING FUNCTIONAL PERFORMANCE STANDARDS

Tasks that fall clearly within your functional responsibility should be covered by performance standards in the form of internal job descriptions. These position descriptions nearly always need revising and updating as a result of your appraisal; if they do not, the appraisal may not have been objective enough. If job descriptions are lacking, of course, they must be developed. In either case, a direct output of the process is a complete set of job descriptions for your function that are specific and up to date. These MBO-type job descriptions contain highly quantified standards of performance for each task; they are quite different from the usual platitudes and "motherhood" statements found on conventional activities-centered job descriptions.

Some tasks that the appraisal turns up as deficient may be the responsibility of another function or a higher management level. Examples would be lack of a supporting document (such as a published policy statement from the executive office) or failure of another department to provide needed informational input. This makes it no less your responsibility, as functional manager, to assure that it is accomplished. It is part of your job to *demand* the support, participation, and cooperation your function requires to meet its objectives; for you to passively accept failure of another function to provide needed support is to share in the failure. Part of your updated job description (and possibly that of one or more of your subordinates) should be the task of obtaining the required information, supporting documentation, or functional support.

It is here that you can distinguish between the *routine tasks* of the function—the "maintenance" type of tasks—and *objectives*, which represent forward progress and improvement. Use of the updated job description to document performance standards for routine tasks also serves the useful purpose of confining objectives to high-priority critical tasks, thus limiting their number.

Properly executed and used, job descriptions serve to secure the productivity gains you have made during a period by documenting the performance standards of jobs until the next upgrading.

HARMONIZING AND RECONCILING GOALS

In an ideal world, you would have complete knowledge of the overall goals of the enterprise, and you would shape your own objectives to accord with these. In a world of perfect communication, you would know exactly what your superior expected of you, and you would tailor your own goals to this knowledge. You would also be fully aware of your colleagues' goals and plans, so your functional objectives would not conflict with theirs.

In the real world of imperfect communication and human fallibility, however, the objectives you set are more likely to be out of phase with those of your associates, your supervisor, and the enterprise as a whole. This does not mean that they should be cast out and redone. Initially your objectives should be somewhat self-centered; it is quite normal and natural for them to be so. They must now go through a process of adjustment, accommodation, and reconciliation to bring them into harmony with those of others.

The next three steps in the process are intended to accomplish this: to progressively modify your functional improvement and personal development objectives to harmonize with those of your colleagues, to adjust them to the needs and goals of your superior, and to accommodate them to the personal aspirations and capabilities of your subordinates. In addition, your objectives will be brought into accord with the overall goals of the organization.

In the course of reshaping your goals, you will have the opportunity to influence the shape and direction of the objectives and plans of the other players in the game.

NOTES

[1] Tosi, Henry L., Rizzo, John, and Carroll, Steven J., Jr., "Setting Goals in MBO," *California Management Review*, Summer 1970.

[2] Sherwin, Douglas S., "Management of Objectives," reprinted by permission of *The Harvard Business Review* (May–June 1976). Copyright by the President and Fellows of Harvard College; all rights reserved.

[3] Mills, Arthur E., *The Dynamics of Management Control Systems*, London Publications, London, 1967.

[4] Shuster, Fred, and Kindall, Alva, "A Survey of the Fortune 500," *Human Resources Management*, Spring 1974.

[5] Babcock, Richard, and Sorensen, P.F., "A Long-Range Approach to MBO," *Management Review*, July 1976. (New York: AMACOM, a division of American Management Associations.)

[6] Babcock, Richard, and Sorensen, P.F., op. cit.

[7] Weihrich, Heinz, "An Uneasy Look at the MBO Jungle," *International Management Review*, April 1976.

HOW TO TRANSLATE
YOUR GOALS
INTO ACTION

FUNCTIONAL IMPROVEMENT PLANNING—
STEP 3 OF THE PROCESS

This step of the process draws upon certain of your high-level management capabilities—those of programming objectives, scheduling and costing-out tasks, and organizing group activities. These are among the most important aspects of managing work. This stage of the process also places demands on management qualities of an even higher order. The first of these is confidence—confidence in yourself and confidence in others—to delegate authority to subordinates. The other is perhaps the most difficult of all the management arts to master: the ability to communicate with others. These qualities are, in the final analysis, the true measures of your qualifications as a manager of people.

If an objective can be envisioned as an end product, this step of the process might be likened to the preparation of a work specification or a set of detailed blueprints that you will be guided by in working toward its completion. Planning is not an easy task; it is a demanding management discipline. Planning requires thoughtful evaluation of available capabilities and resources, reasoned selection from among alternative ways to achieve a result, and unremitting attention to detail.

Planning is an essential condition to the accomplishment of objectives. It is highly unlikely that any achievement of any consequence involving groups of people was ever made without a plan. There are managers, sad to say, who regard planning with distaste and consider it an activity that takes up time better spent *doing* things.

It cannot be stressed often enough that objectives alone are not sufficient to move the enterprise forward, regardless

**CHAPTER
EIGHT**

of how inspirational they may appear or sound. Objectives must be backed by solid evidence of *commitment* that the actions necessary to achieve your declared goals (1) have been thought through, and (2) will be taken. This is the purpose of the improvement plans in Section D of the matrix.

This critical step represents both an opportunity and a danger. The danger is that you will be pressured by time and job constraints to set up your improvement plans and assign tasks independently of the job and personal development goals of your subordinates. The opportunity is the occasion to bring your subordinates into the process of management by objectives and self-control as full participants.

To avoid the danger and capitalize on the opportunity, each major task of a plan should be coordinated with the objectives of the subordinate to whom it is assigned. In theory, your task assignment becomes *the subordinate's objective*—neat and simple in theory, but difficult and complicated in practice. Trade-offs must be made between what you feel should be done and the capabilities, needs, and desires of subordinates. These concessions must be made at every level of the process. They are accommodations which go to the heart of the human values central to the process. To make these accommodations requires a good deal of give-and-take and a receptivity to the requirements of others. These are the same qualities you look for from your own boss when you are negotiating with him or her on your objectives, of course, so it's a case of "doing unto others." Failure on your part to make these concessions will subvert the process.

On the other hand, the compromises you make will pay a high return on investment in terms of more mature and more self-reliant subordinates to whom you can delegate authority with confidence. Each objective, if it is to be achieved, must be supported by a definitive and detailed action plan (in Section D of the matrix). In order to ensure accomplishment of the plans, each step in each plan must contain essentials, as follows:

THE FIVE ESSENTIAL PLAN ELEMENTS

1. *Firm assignment of responsibility* for taking the action. Assignment must always be to an individual—not to a section, group, or department—and should represent delegation of authority to the maximum extent consistent with company policy.

2. *The timing of each step*, expressed as a planned completion date (end-of-month dates are preferable, but too many year-end target dates may be indicative of weak commitment). These dates serve as milestones for your progress reporting during implementation of the plans.

3. *Identification of additional resources needed:* workers, capabilities, facilities, equipment, computer time and capacity, outside services, and support from other functions.

4. *The estimated dollar costs* of each major step, in terms of both operating expenses and capital investment in facilities and equipment.

5. *An estimate of the benefits* to be derived from accomplishment, in terms of income from increased revenues, improved product margins, or reduced costs and expenses. (It must be recognized that certain improvements to meet legal or social obligations, such as equal employment opportunity plans, for example, may be difficult to express in these terms.)

Your improvement plan must be programmed and expressed in hard terms of real action—as tasks, not as soft intentions or "wish lists." Your plans should be stated on the matrix in concise highlight fashion (they can be detailed in other supporting documents).

You should assign responsibility and delegate authority for each task on the action plan to an individual. Without such delegation and assignment your plan is virtually meaningless; chances are it will not be accomplished. Similarly, each task must have a specific date for completion (starting dates are not useful, in the writer's view, but may be shown if desired). In this connection, frequent use of year-end dates, "12/31/ ," is a device often used to avoid accountability for the task and should be avoided.

Each step in each plan must be clear and specific and be expressed in terms of results. To assure this, the first words in each should be active verbs. For example, a plan to improve the function of product reliability and quality might read, in part:

- *Train* two design engineers in the principles and techniques of reliability engineering.
- *Establish and staff* a quality assurance function reporting to plant manager.
- *Set up* departmental quality control charts with min-max limits.

Cost savings resulting from improvement plans should be estimated for each identifiable item of labor, materials, and expenses, in terms of current-year savings and annualized savings for future years. The costs of new resources needed to implement the action plans should be estimated in like fashion; operating expenses for added personnel, purchased services, leased equipment, and internal support from service departments should be expressed as current-year expenses and annualized expenses. Costs of new facilities and equipment should be designated as capital costs.

HOW TO CREATE COORDINATION WITH OTHERS

THE PEER REVIEW— STEP 4 OF THE PROCESS

This step is a key element in the complex and never-ending process of reconciling and adjusting your objectives and plans to the needs, goals, and plans of the other managers of the organization with whom you relate—your subordinates, colleagues, and organizational superiors—and to the goals, policies, norms and values of the enterprise as a whole.

In the previous chapter, the necessity to make concessions and accommodations to the needs and capabilities of your subordinates was discussed. There is a similar necessity to reconcile your goals and plans to those of your peers on the same organizational level. It is equally to your benefit to do so.

It is natural and normal to set objectives and develop plans that will advance your own functional interests. On occasion, these can run head-on into the self-centered goals and plans of other managers, and conflict can result. In an ideal world, both managers would amend their proposals to eliminate the contention. In practice, however, the more dominant manager usually concedes the least, often causing the less assertive manager to regret yielding to the other. No system or process, however effective, is going to change this kind of human behavior, of course; all it can do is provide a mechanism whereby the aggrieved party can appeal to a higher authority. This mechanism is provided by Step 5 of the process (discussed in the next chapter), in which any unresolved disputes between managers about goals and plans are carried over for review and adjudication by the managers' superior.

It is unrealistic, even naive, to expect that team spirit or a cooperative attitude

CHAPTER NINE

among colleagues alone will cause managers to modify their self-centered objectives and plans in the interests of organizational integration and coordination. Harmonizing the goals and plans of managers of different functions requires active effort and an organized process.

COORDINATION THROUGH COMMUNICATION

The key element is communication. During the process of developing objectives and action plans, every manager is required to keep fellow managers on the same organizational level informed through regular meetings and formal interchange of draft documents. It is vitally important, for instance, that an administrative manager be informed about a proposed new sales-incentive plan or the plan for a new Midwestern sales office early in the game, so its effect on the administrative workload can be assessed. Similarly, the sales manager should know about a proposed change in the order processing system that will affect the way sales representatives write up customer orders.

If you are a manager whose function is to provide services and support to other functions—services such as computer data processing, communications, marketing services, accounting controls, and administrative services—you are enabled through this process to calculate the aggregate demand that will be made upon your resources by your colleagues during the coming year. Your own objectives and plans can then reflect your response to these demands. Should the demand for services exceed your functional capacity, the requesting functions may be told to look outside the organization or to scale down their plans to fit; if neither is practicable, your capacity may have to be expanded.

The peer reviews also help to prevent suboptimization of functional goals, plans, and resource allocation. This is an ever-present danger in large, decentralized organizations, especially those that lack good communication between functions. Not infrequently, a company can suffer from a malady known among performing artists as "deformation professionelle" (commonly denoted by the overdeveloped leg muscles of ballet dancers). An organization whose chief executive has a strong engineering background, for instance, may give such heavy support and recognition to the technical department that the organization becomes functionally unbalanced. The marketing and production functions, in this situation, may end up with the short end of the resource-allocation stick. The management by contract process may not be able to cure this disease, but it surely can help to expose it to view.

THE DANGER OF DAMAGING COMPETITIVENESS

The interchange of drafts of objectives and improvement plans can be expected to generate some spirited debate and disagreement. For this *not* to occur would be quite abnormal—an indication of organizational apathy perhaps. Discussion and disagreement between managers can bring about constructive changes in functional objectives and plans, the effects of which are improved coordination and integration—or, conceivably, even a measure of that overused term, "synergism." Carried to extremes, however (and this must be guarded against), the disputes between functions can become a kind of damaging competitiveness, a destructive internecine combat for larger shares of available resources. Again, the management by contract process may not put a stop to such counterproductive activity, but it can serve to make the bad actors visible.

Inevitably, as noted earlier, there will be some unresolved conflicts remaining between colleagues. Issues of overlapping jurisdiction arising from disagreement on functional boundaries, duplication of activities, or conflicting interpretations of corporate policies and procedures may have to be resolved by the department head during the next step in the process, the review and negotiation phase.

HOW TO GET YOUR
SHARE OF RESOURCES

REVIEW AND NEGOTIATION—
STEP 5 OF THE PROCESS

This step of the process could be called a "moment of truth." It involves a person-to-person dialogue between you and your boss, out of which you intend to emerge with your proposed objectives and improvement plans endorsed. Your earlier preparations should have armed you well for the encounter. You should be equipped with the results of an intensive functional self-appraisal, a list of objectives that has survived review by your peer associates, a thoughtful plan of improvement action, and confidence in your ability to win your boss's blessing. Your initiative in preparing this *discussion agenda* should have given you a strong advantage in the negotiations that now take place—the advantage that comes from doing one's homework well—and a measure of control over the outcome.

Use of the terms "encounter" and "negotiating advantage" may convey the impression that the review and negotiation step represents a *conflict* between two antagonists conducted in an atmosphere of hostility. To the contrary, this step should be viewed as a productive process. It represents, to be sure, a kind of turnabout situation—one in which you, as subordinate, take the initiative to identify what must be done to make your function a more productive contributor to the enterprise and then proceed to force your objectives on your superior. (The term "force" is used in the sense of influence, persuade, induce, or otherwise engage your boss in the effort.) It is not only your right to enlist your boss's support in the effort to reach the goals you believe in—it is your *obligation*. It should be pointed out that his or her authority is not diminished but is strengthened by the turnabout.

At all times during this process you are competing with other managers for your

**CHAPTER
TEN**

share of the firm's resources. *The management by contract process is part of the process of allocating resources.* Resources are always limited—always less than the aggregate demands upon them. Should resources exceed aggregate demand, the organization is not utilizing them efficiently. One of the limited resources you are competing for is a share of your boss's attention, and the negotiating sessions you are now participating in are among the demands on the boss's time. You are now doing a selling job; the more persuasive your proposal, the more compelling your objectives, and the more convincing your improvement plans, the better your chances are of getting his or her endorsement and committed support.

Assuming that you have done a serious job on the first three steps of the process, you have by now demonstrated your capability:

1. To isolate those areas within your function that need management attention
2. To define your problems and identify opportunities
3. To set challenging objectives for your function
4. To select from among promising alternative strategies to achieve them
5. To plan a productive course of improvement action
6. To determine what additional resources you need to carry out your plans
7. To set up your self-control limits—that is, to identify in what aspects of your job a close and continuous relationship with your boss is needed, and in what aspects you feel you need little supervision

In Step 4 you carried on a productive discussion with the managers of other functions with which your function relates. As a result you have undoubtedly modified your objectives and improvement plans to bring them into closer harmony with theirs—even as they should have reconciled theirs in some respects to yours.

THE MATRIX—AGENDA FOR NEGOTIATION

The output of the work you have done—the information you have gathered, organized, and analyzed; the discussions you have held with your subordinates and your peers; and the intensive thinking you have done about your function and its role in the organization— should have now been synthesized into a concise highlight summary on your Objectives and Improvement Matrix (or similar format). This is the vehicle designed to convey your proposed objectives and improvement plans to your boss. This is the form that now serves as the discussion agenda for this and subsequent meetings. This is the document that becomes a contract upon approval by your boss.

THE NEGOTIATION PROCESS

Your immediate goal is to obtain endorsement and approval of your proposal. It is unrealistic, however, to expect that your proposal will be blessed on the basis of a single meeting with your boss. It is more likely that a series of meetings will be needed to resolve all of the issues and complexities raised by you and the other managers reporting to your boss. Probably the most critical of these is the matter of goals compatibility.

In MBO theory each functional manager establishes objectives within a known context of the greater goals of the enterprise as a whole—individual objectives are thus consonant and compatible with corporate goals. It follows, then, that the objectives of the various managers are in harmony with each other.

In practice, however, the overall goals of the organization are not always clear and consistent, nor are they always perfectly communicated to lower-level managers. Even in organizations with superior communications, different managers may have quite different perceptions of what the corporate goals really are. What is more, in the process of functional goal setting, a manager may lose sight of the broader objectives of the enterprise while striving to set goals that meet other criteria; compatibility and harmony are the qualities that may end up in short supply.

In business life, as in private life, managers are driven by self-interest. In setting functional goals, they will quite naturally be biased toward those which tend to enhance their career advancement potential, challenge their professional capabilities, and provide them with the greatest personal satisfaction. This need not be incompatible with the greater good of the organization. Odiorne observed wryly that if the personal development goals and the corporate goals "were antithetical the system would be self-destructing."[1]

What is needed, of course, is a process that reconciles the person-focused objectives of individual managers with the larger goals of the enterprise—Rensis Likert's "self-actualization"—and at the same time brings the sometimes divergent goals of the various managers into harmony with one another. To accomplish this without riding roughshod over the individual manager's initiative and sensibilities is perhaps the most difficult, demanding, and delicate task in the whole management process. The peer review just described does part of the job by bringing peer pressure upon a manager whenever that individual's goals appear to represent damaging competition for an unfair share of available resources. Chapter 8 described the process of coordinating and accommodating your plans to the goals of your subordinates. This is another phase of the continuous and never-ending process of reconciling and harmonizing the objectives of people on various organization levels and in different functions. The rest of the task requires face-to-face review and negotiation between the superior and the subordinate managers.

The review and negotiation are conducted in the context of:

- The superior's privileged information about the company's business development strategies, potential organizational changes, financial capabilities, and capital resources
- The objectives and improvement plans of the other subordinate managers who report directly
- Knowledge of the management strengths and weaknesses of these subordinates

During the review process, your objectives and plans, as well as those of the other managers, usually will be amended to avoid any remaining duplications of effort and conflicts between managers, to cover tasks that may not have been included by any manager, to adjust objectives to individual managers' capabilities, and to scale plans to resources that realistically can be anticipated. Any objectives that are clearly out of joint with overall corporate goals can be brought into line at this time.

In the course of reviewing your objectives and improvement plans, your department head may determine that your perception of your responsibility is faulty, or that it does not accord with higher objectives. The superior may conclude that your self-analysis was not sufficiently objective or may discern that you have omitted a task that is considered critical to the department during the coming year. Similarly, your supervisor may find that you are focusing your attention on tasks that are less vital to overall company results but may be more gratifying to you in the professional sense.

This is the boss's opportunity to eliminate overlapping and duplications, to harmonize goals, to fill in important gaps in the overall effort, and to help each manager set critical priorities. It is also the stage at which your supervisor will advise you and your fellow managers of impending new programs, major changes in policy, and new opportunities that he or she is aware of through direct contact with higher executive echelons. These new factors must be incorporated into your plans. This review also enables the department head to see the requirements of all managers for resources in their aggregate and thus to determine whether they are available or can be afforded. To the degree that requirements exceed attainable resources, demands may have to be scaled down. This may require a reiteration in which the effects of any such cutbacks are assessed by the affected managers and plans revised.

At this stage, too, the superior often has to reaffirm each manager's decision limits and discretion areas. As explained by Tosi, Rizzo, and Carroll, it is important "to spell out areas in which the subordinate has some latitude so that he knows what his decision limits are. Otherwise he may be misled into believing that he can participate in departmental and organization decisions that have been defined, either procedurally or by management fiat, as being outside his discretion area."[2]

NEGOTIATING LEADERSHIP STYLES

Another vitally important aspect of your job should be brought up for discussion in these negotiating sessions with your boss. This is the issue of the leadership role that you feel your superior should assume for each of your principal objectives. It was pointed out earlier (Chapter 3) that a boss may have to employ a variety of leadership styles depending on a subordinate's maturity—experience, technical skill, job know-how, and confidence—in relation to each task. In Section 3 of the matrix form, you should indicate by means of a code number or letter the degree of task instruction and the extent of ongoing contact and facilitation you require on each objective.

This is a legitimate issue for negotiation between you, because you and your superior may hold very different perceptions of the difficulties involved in accomplishing certain of your objectives; these differences can be reconciled, at least to some extent, in this process. In a very real sense, also, you are establishing through this process your own self-control limits.

During the negotiations, your department head may take issue with the leadership style that you have proposed on a particular goal. Your supervisor may feel that you are not experienced enough in a particular task to warrant a hands-off mode of leadership and so may propose a change to one of closer involvement. If this is agreed to, your superior's close relationship during performance of the plan will be perceived as supportive rather than threatening and thus will be welcomed.

Hersey and Blanchard have developed a "task-relationship matrix" (illustrated below) to express leadership styles:[3]

HIGH

3 High Relationship Low Task	2 High Task High Relationship
4 Low Relationship Low Task	1 High Task Low Relationship

RELATIONSHIP BEHAVIOR

LOW   HIGH

TASK BEHAVIOR

The quadrant numbers 1 to 4 may be used to indicate the respective styles in the final column of Section C on the matrix.

The revising of objectives and action plans is accomplished through a combination of individual negotiations and group discussion. It is essentially a process of trade-offs between desires and reality—a process that has been described by Earl Hilburn, president of Western Union Corporation, as one of "equalizing the dissatisfaction" among a group of managers in competition for shares of the total resources available. These negotiations are particularly critical to the process—indeed, Weihrich and Wether in "Refining MBO through Negotiation" observe that "the most difficult part of setting objectives is in the interrelationship between superior and subordinate during negotiation of objectives . . . no dimension of MBO is as crucial as the face-to-face encounter between them."[4]

Awareness on the part of both manager and boss that the results of these discussions and negotiations will be incorporated into a contract between the two parties can bring to the process a degree of intensity and realism that is all too often missing from the discussion of objectives in the conventional MBO program.

NOTES

[1] Odiorne, George, "MBO and the Phenomenon of Goals Displacement," *Human Resource Management*, Spring 1974.

[2] Tosi, Henry L., Rizzo, John, and Carroll, Steven J., Jr., "Setting Goals in MBO," *California Management Review*, Summer, 1970.

[3] Hersey, Paul, and Blanchard, Kenneth H.,"What's Missing in MBO." *Management Review*, October 1977. (New York: AMACOM, a division of American Management Associations.)

[4] Weihrich, Heinz, and Wether, William B., Jr., "Refining MBO Through Negotiations," *MSU Business Topics*, Summer 1975. Reprinted by permission of publisher, Division of Research, Graduate School of Business Administration, Michigan State University.

HOW TO DOCUMENT
THE AGREEMENT

THE MANAGEMENT CONTRACT—
STEP 6 OF THE PROCESS

This phase of the process is more a *milestone* than a step; more a *result* than an action. The management contract is the output of a series of related actions, the product of a process—one that has involved a great deal of effort, initiative, productive debate, and insightful analysis by you, your associates, and your subordinates. This process has been capped in Step 5 by a series of constructive person-to-person negotiating and trade-off sessions with your boss.

In terms of the metaphor used earlier, which depicted the process as an upward-spiraling stairway each step of which takes you higher and closer to your objectives, the contract represents a midpoint landing that you have reached through your efforts. This agreement between you and your organizational superior is a documentation of the understanding that now exists in your respective minds as to the nature of your job, the extent of your responsibilities, your expected contribution to the organization, and your committed goals for the near-term future. It also documents the understanding between you as to the obligations of your boss to support you with resources and leadership in your progress toward these goals.

There is strong unanimity among students of management that lack of such mutual understanding is one of the more serious impediments to full productivity of the enterprise, for managers tend to make bold decisions and take productive risks with confidence only when individual decision limits are clearly known and only when they are reasonably sure of the superior's support. And managers will initiate action with assurance only when they have confidence that subordinates know and understand their roles and will perform them well.

There is some evidence that complete understanding between manager and

**CHAPTER
ELEVEN**

superviser is quite rare; that even when it has been achieved, it tends to degrade with time and the pressures of the job. You will recall George Odiorne's observation, noted in an earlier chapter, that subordinates and superiors tend to agree on only 10 percent of the goals that subordinates consider important. The contract serves as a mechanism to preserve the understanding that has been reached and to record major changes as they occur. The agreement is an important indicator of progress toward a new and more constructive relationship—a productive partnership—between you and your boss. This relationship, all too frequently, is an adversary one, or one of dominance, and the contract is symbolic of a profound change to a relationship of mutual interdependence and mutual support—of shared power and shared commitment to the same goals.

Viewed in terms of the steps already taken the contract can be seen as the completion of a firm base of support for the new relationship. Looking ahead to the final four steps of the process, the contract can be viewed as the foundation of a more productive association between you as you jointly work toward mutual goals.

WHAT THE CONTRACT MEANS
TO YOU AS SUBORDINATE

Approval by your boss of your proposed Objectives and Improvement Matrix has now converted the document into a contract between you. This contract reflects the results of the negotiations and trade-offs— the modifications you have made to accommodate the needs and values of your superior and the reshaping of your objectives to the overall goals, policies, values, norms, and culture of the firm. The "fit" of your objectives with the larger goals can never be a perfect one—and it is a mistake to seek perfection. The test in this regard, as it is in many others, is the test of reasonableness.

The contract imposes upon you a firm and binding obligation to direct your full management capabilities and efforts toward the achievement of the agreed-upon objectives. This obligation cannot be taken lightly. Your boss, by agreeing with your objectives and improvement plans, has demonstrated confidence in your ability to manage your function now and in the period ahead.

By delegating authority to you through the contract mechanism— that is, by providing you with the resources you require—your superior has also shown a high degree of faith and trust in you to protect these resources and manage them well. By concurring in the management style you have proposed, by agreeing to minimize task instructions and to limit ongoing involvement, your boss has demonstrated belief in your job maturity and ability to control your own activities.

WHAT THE CONTRACT MEANS
TO YOU AS SUPERVISOR

When you approve the Objectives and Improvement Matrix forms of your subordinates, you are entering into a binding contractual relationship with each of them. Do not forget that you are "doing unto others as you would have done unto you." Just as you expect your boss to treat you with respect and regard for personal worth and to exhibit toward you the qualities of confidence and trust, you are exhibiting these qualities toward those who report to you when you agree to support their objectives, provide them with resources, delegate decision authority, and allow them a large measure of job self-control. You are not doing this out of the goodness of your heart; you are doing it in your own enlightened self-interest, because it is the most productive method to achieve your own personal and company-related goals. That it also serves your subordinates well is a not inconsiderable benefit.

WHAT THE CONTRACT MEANS
TO YOUR SUBORDINATES

The contract should be represented to your subordinates as a unique opportunity to develop their own management skills to the extent that their individual desires and capabilities permit, to participate in a meaningful way in the organization's decision-making processes, and to identify with (and contribute to) the larger goals of the enterprise. Even more important to the more mature of your subordinates, it offers the opportunity to exercise a greater degree of self-control on the job. Not everyone wants this, to be sure. A subordinate who is not psychologically conditioned for such responsibility should not be deprived of needed emotional security. The contract provides a measure of this security by ensuring that you share with your subordinate responsibility and accountability for the task.

WHAT THE CONTRACT MEANS
TO THE ENTERPRISE

George Odiorne repeatedly cautions against the tendency to regard the MBO process as a paper exercise, an exchange of a piece of paper rather than a face-to-face managerial system. In the process described here, the exchange of paper is a triggering mechanism designed to stimulate person-to-person and group discussion and debate. In this system, human values are central, but the paper forms and documents serve several essential purposes.

- Committing objectives and plans to paper forces a manager to seek out information, analyze and organize it, and cast out nonessential data. It is an exercise in self-knowledge.

- The paper forms that are exchanged among managers act as agenda for productive discourse; they help to confine discussion to relevant matters, and they record the results of this face-to-face communication.

- The resulting documents—the management contracts between each manager and organizational superior—are the product of person-to-person discussion, debate, often disagreement. In the course of this interchange, personal viewpoints can be expanded, new insights gained, and a greater measure of understanding reached between subordinate and supervisor.

- At all times, and at every stage of the process, the paper forms are only *symbols* of the personal relationships between managers on different organization levels and between colleagues on the same level.

- The process of progressively modifying objectives and improvement plans through accommodations and concessions with other managers—first with subordinates, then with peer managers, and finally with superiors—is a paper process. The output of the process is a synchronized network of goals and plans that represents a high degree of harmony, collaboration, and synergism among the various managers of the enterprise. The effect of this might be likened to that of a laser, which takes the scattered rays of light and concentrates them into a focused beam of enormous power.

HOW TO "GET THERE" THROUGH SELF-MANAGEMENT

IMPLEMENTATION OF YOUR PLAN—
STEP 7 OF THE PROCESS

The effect of the contractual agreement is that you and your boss now *share* responsibility to perform the tasks necessary to achieve functional objectives; you *share* in the credit for accomplishment, and you also *share* in accountability for failure. Neither of you is allowed to disclaim responsibility to take the actions you have committed to take; neither of you is entitled to claim credit for the other's accomplishments; and neither of you may walk away from failure while pointing a finger of blame at the other. The actions of both of you during implementation are guided and governed by the terms of the contract, embodied in the matrix which lists your objectives and approved action plans.

- Your actions are guided and governed by your contractual obligation to perform the actions and to meet the time and cost schedules in the plan.
- The actions of your superior are guided and governed by the contractual obligation to provide the budget funds, physical resources, management support, and leadership specified in the document.

Implicit in the agreement is the obligation of both parties *not* to take any action that will prevent the plans from being effectively implemented or to divert resources away from their approved purpose. There is a further implication that knowledge of any event or development which threatens the successful implementation of the plans must be shared promptly. Similarly, knowledge about new techniques and improved processes that could conceivably accelerate plan schedules, reduce costs, or increase benefits should be communicated promptly.

CHAPTER TWELVE

The implementation phase of the process covers the duration of the contract period, generally 1 year. During this period, in your role as functional manager, you are entrusted with authority to manage a portion, however small, of the firm's resources. For the duration of this phase, you have assumed the responsibility to perform the particular function effectively. And you have accepted the accountability for results, good or bad, that goes with authority. As a participant in this management process called management by contract, you have taken on the further obligation to achieve, during this period, a set of objectives that will raise the performance standards and increase the productivity of your function while at the same time enhancing the competitive effectiveness of the total organization.

A condition of your participation in the process is its implied promise to benefit you in several ways. One, it promises to develop your capabilities as a manager, thereby enhancing your ability to take on greater responsibility. Two, it promises to provide you with the personal gratification that comes from achievement. Three, it promises to make your accomplishments more visible to those who control the organization's reward system.

Your earlier work, leading to the contract agreement, has set the stage for this critical phase of the process. If you have done it well, you now have a well-defined mission, firm objectives, and a clear blueprint—your plan—to guide you. These have all been coordinated with others and approved by your superior. It is in the implementation phase that your contribution to the enterprise can bring you these rewards. Now it's up to you. Your ability to control your own efforts and to cope with the change that is inevitable as you proceed is the key element for success.

SELF-CONTROL AND SELF-MANAGEMENT

As a manager-member of a functional organization or a project, you are an important contributor to the results of the group. The primary output of the organization, of course, is products and services that fulfill economic and social needs. An even more essential output is *positive cash flow* on which the enterprise can thrive and grow. In a third important respect, the output is *a high return on invested capital*, realized through productive utilization of the firm's resources.

As a functional manager, you have two jobs—a *job to do* and a *job to manage*. The management by contract process is a system for *managing your job.* The process assumes that you are a mature, competent, and energetic manager with the professional skill to perform your job well; the process is intended to help you plan it, organize it, control it, and improve its output.

This stage of the process involves both doing and managing. You are now managing the doing of the job: controlling and measuring performance of people, comparing results to a plan, and modulating your activities to cope with unanticipated events. An old sales bromide says, "Plan your work and work your plan." Sound advice, of course, but in working any plan, it comes into contact with the real world and is swiftly affected by changing circumstances.

Your performance in anticipating and coping with events and in controlling your function through the turbulence of rapid change is the measure of your managerial capabilities. The knowledge that you are in control of your job—because you have done the hard work of analyzing, organizing, and planning it—plus the assurance that you will be provided with control reports and feedback on actual performance will enable you to proceed through this implementation phase with confidence. The capability to make your own control decisions during this phase, with a minimum of intervention by higher management, can be an important source of gratification to you. And the assurance that your boss is equally committed to your objectives and shares with you the responsibility to achieve them can be a comforting thought when the going gets rough.

Self-control in this sense is the furthest thing from license to "do your thing" without restraint or guidance from others. I prefer to call it "self-management." What it means is freedom to control your own activities within certain well-defined constraints: first, the constraints of an approved end-result or objective to which you are fully committed; second, the constraints of an approved plan or program which you have had a significant role in formulating. Self-control permits you to modulate your actions based on your own evaluation of (1) feedback information on performance, and (2) information on events and developments that can affect your plans and objectives.

During the objective-setting stage of the process, you were required to specify the leadership style you wanted your boss to follow for each major objective. By so doing, you were establishing your own self-control limits. By specifying a limited-control role for your boss, you were effectively enlarging your own area of self-control. In the negotiation stage that followed, to be sure, he or she may have overruled you and retained a larger measure of control on tasks for which it was felt you were not fully equipped; nonetheless, you had a voice in the process of defining your respective control limits.

HOW TO COPE
WITH CHANGE

FEEDBACK AND RESPONSE—
STEP 8 OF THE PROCESS

During the implementation period, the actyons of both you and your organizational superior are further guided and modified by regular periodic control reports issued by the controller and other "scorekeeping" functions: by the functions in close contact with customers, such as marketing, sales, and customer service; and by the functions responsible for relations with the other constituencies of the firm, such as industrial relations, government relations, public relations, and investor relations. These reports are essential to keep the process flexible and adaptive to change. Reports are of two basic types:

1. Control "feedback" reports on performance of your functionpas regards revenue, cost, and expense budgets, performance standards, quality goals, cost-reduction targets, and other significant internal bunchmarks
2. Control reports on external events, developments, and trends in markets, competition, technology, government regulation and legislation, and the socioeconomic environment

Information contained in the first type of report can alter the actions of both parties, even modify the plan in extreme cases, but should not affect the basic contract. External forces can have an impact on company strategies, on the organizational structure, or on company policies that is serious enough to demand changes in plans.

At some point, to be sure, the cumulative effect of external events will undoubtedly demand that your plans be revised. That this *will* happen is inevitable; *when* it will happen, however, is beyond human capability to predict.

**CHAPTER
THIRTEEN**

NO PLAN SURVIVES CONTACT
WITH REALITY

A popular (but oversimplified) conception of "objective" is that it represents a desired destination. Unfortunately, the time it takes to get there and the cost of the journey are important factors not considered in this management cliché. A good plan can be likened to an itinerary that specifies the shortest distance, the quickest time, and the least cost for the trip. Experience tells us that, once embarked on a journey, it may be necessary on occasion to detour from the favored route to a different route because of roadblocks and other travel hazards.

A destination, once selected, remains fixed—it is not normally changed simply because a particular road is closed. So it is with objectives and plans; an objective, once set, should not be changed except in unusual circumstances. A plan, on the other hand, can and will change. A plan, in fact, *must* change, must constantly renew itself, if it is to remain viable.

Every plan is an exercise in futures. The only things certain about the future are (1) that it is unknowable and (2) that it will be different from what we expect. No matter how skillful you are as a planner— no matter how clear your crystal ball appears—unforeseen and unforeseeable events will in time cause the best of plans to become obsolete. For this reason, you must remain flexible and adaptable as you implement your plans. These occurrences can affect your chosen course of action for better or for worse, depending on whether they represent opportunities or threats. Conceivably, they can be both. They should not, however, alter your objectives—provided that your objectives are soundly based.

Marketing management may, for example, find its plan to increase its share of available market blocked by the action of a competitor who has moved unexpectedly into a particular market area with an attractive new product. If management should persist in following the plan to invest large advertising expenditures in this market, it might find the budget overspent while the market share remains unchanged. A change of plan to shift the funds to another market area could prove to be more productive.

There is something of a paradox here; the manager who remains adaptable and ready to modify the plan stands a better chance of reaching the objective than one who rigidly follows a plan without ever deviating from it.

Of what use, then, is the plan? If the plan is to become obsolete before it is fully implemented, why bother to prepare the plan in the first instance? Simply this—it is the *act of planning* that produces the real benefits. The process, not the document, is the product. It is a process of *identifying* alternative courses of action and *selecting* from among them the ones that have the greatest promise of success; *programming* these into specific action steps that can be costed out, scheduled, and assigned to individuals as tasks; and *measuring and controlling* these tasks.

The documented plan represents a foundation for flexibility in action, a base course from which you can deviate with assurance that you know from whence you came. If you lack a plan, you might not even know that you are diverging, much less in which direction. If your plan contains good benchmarks and milestones, you can even measure the *amount* of deviation from your established course.

MANAGING CHANGE

Many managers are attracted by problems, and honestly believe that their ability to arrive at ingenious solutions is the real measure of their management capabilities. They believe, moreover, that by managing in a problem-solving mode they are coping with new situations as they develop, that they are *managing change*. For a manager to devote a major share of time and energy to solving problems and correcting weaknesses, however, is to focus on the past; the present remains undermanaged and the future is neglected. Today's problems are almost always the consequences of last year's failure to plan and manage; the difficulties are compounded when yesterday's mistakes are allowed to consume management's energies today. Infatuation with problem solving can also lead to assignment of the best people to the worst problems while the most promising opportunities go unattended. It is often better to look upon the sins and errors of the past as "sunk costs" of the business and to leave them out of the calculation of return on effort expended. In this way, management's full energies can be directed toward strengthening strong points, capitalizing on past successes, and building on proven performance for the future.

Solving problems is the furthest thing from managing change; it is reacting to events. Managing change is more a process of *problem prevention*—analogous perhaps to quality assurance in industry, which seeks to prevent product defects *before* they occur rather than to correct them afterward by rework. It is a process of anticipating change, controlling it, and directing it to your advantage.

The first requirement for managing change is a plan. The second is a free and copious flow of information about what is going on both within your function and elsewhere. The third requirement is a method for processing information—for identifying which information is significant to you. The 80/20 rule is at work here—you need a method for picking out of a mass of data the 20 percent most meaningful so you can discard the 80 percent that is less useful.

As you proceed to carry out your plans, you can expect that they will be beset with constant change. They will be affected, first, by changes that take place within the organization. Second, they are bound to be impacted by events and developments in the outside world, where change is ever present. Third, your plans inevitably will be affected by Murphy's famous law, which says that whatever *can* go wrong *will* go wrong.

CONTRACT AMENDMENTS

As in any other contractual arrangement between two parties, there must be some provision for reopening and renegotiating the terms of the contract, as circumstances and conditions change over time. The mechanism for this need not be complex, but some discipline is needed to prohibit either party from making amendments for self-serving purposes or to avoid accountability for nonperformance.

Normally renegotiation should be permitted, given sufficient cause, during regularly scheduled performance reviews (probably at three-month intervals). The contract should be reopened only as a result of noncontrollable factors that may have an effect on the expressed obligations of either party, external events which normally cannot be anticipated, such as:

- Customer cancellation of a large order or contract or the unexpected booking of a large order or contract not included in the sales forecast
- A major move by a competitor, such as an important new product introduction or entry into the company's markets (should have been anticipated by marketing, of course)
- An unexpected governmental action affecting the company
- A strike, or a disaster such as storm or fire
- Illness or accident
- The cumulative effect of many changes over a prolonged period of time

Internal actions normally should not provide grounds for changing the contract. Organization changes should be anticipated insofar as possible and provided for in objectives and plans; this is not always possible, however, because of their sensitive nature.

During early stages of the program, the promise dates for completion of objectives or action plans may be unrealistic. Many managers will tend to overcommit, and it is not always possible, nor always desirable, to correct this tendency during the initial negotiations. Managers should not be required to live with the consequences of their inexperience with MBO and eagerness to please the boss, however, so a degree of tolerance should be provided in the first few performance reviews. The program matrix provides space for a revised date to be entered at time of change.

HOW TO GET CREDIT
FOR YOUR GAINS

PROGRESS REPORTING—
STEP 9 OF THE PROCESS

This step in the process is actually an ongoing repetitive task rather than a single step. At the close of each month during the period covered by your objectives and improvement plans, you should prepare and issue a progress report covering your performance during the month.

In the self-control process presented here, every monthly progress report is the basis for a performance self-review. Each of your progress reports is a record of your performance on specific tasks in your improvement plans; these are inextricably linked to your objectives. Thus each progress report is a record of your progression and advancement toward your objectives. It is helpful to summarize several monthly reports into a periodic summary—say quarterly— for the specific purpose of joint review with your boss; the broader management perspective gained as a result of this review can be beneficial to both of you.

GETTING RECOGNITION FOR
YOUR ACCOMPLISHMENTS

Progress reports are the principal vehicle for recording and tracking your own progress during implementation of your plans. Progress reports are also an important means for calling on to problems that may require resolution on a higher level or intervention by a higher executive. They serve, too, as a method to call the attention of higher management to opportunities that are beyond the capabilities of the reporting function, that require coordinated efforts by several functions, or that may need additional resources.

**CHAPTER
FOURTEEN**

They are also a superb medium for ensuring that you will get recognition and credit for your accomplishments. Some bosses have short memories; they forget last year's contribution and ask, "What have you done for me lately?" Most of us have known the type of boss who takes credit for every new idea, discovery, and accomplishment by subordinates. And it's not unknown for a boss to take the name of the author off the report and replace it with his or her own when sending it upstairs. A regular progress report, with your name on it, can prevent this petty thievery and help you to retain the credit for your own achievements.

COMMUNICATION THROUGH PROGRESS REPORTING

It is vitally important for an organization that is structured along functional lines to have a method and a discipline to convey information across these lines. Meetings, of course, are one method. Multifunctional teams or task groups are useful when employed on specific projects or problems. In the conventional hierarchy, however, information frequently must move upward to a crossover level, then downward again—an inefficient process in which a good deal of content can be lost.

How can such an organization ensure that each function has ongoing, up-to-date information on the activities, problems, and priorities of the other functions with which it interrelates? Obviously, there is no substitute for continuous daily open contact and communication among people at all levels between functions; this, however, does not always exist, and as the organization grows in size this becomes more and more time-consuming. The exchange of managers' weekly and monthly *progress reports* has been found to be an effective way to bridge this communication gap. The requirement that every functional manager prepare a formal progress report each week and each month forces them to set aside a few hours regularly to review activities and organize them into a coherent report of progress on the tasks, projects, and programs with which each is concerned. In the process of reviewing the immediate past, the manager is forced to rethink priorities for the near-term future.

The process of committing accomplishments to paper helps the manager to crystalize aims and goals. It tends to prevent backsliding—having taken credit for an achievement, a manager is understandably reluctant to rescind it. (It is not unknown for a manager to claim completion of a task before it is finished, usually in the sincere belief that it will be completed before anyone will check on it.)

Managers who receive progress reports from several direct reports often find areas of potential conflict, duplications of effort, or failure to cover some areas adequately. Requiring managers to prepare summary progress reports that will be read, in turn, by their superiors ensures that they will take steps to resolve the conflicts, eliminate the duplications, and fill the gaps.

Requiring managers, further, to send copies of their functional progress reports to associates in the other functions provides the organization with a superb interfunctional communications medium. It's not unusual for Edna Engineering to find out that Marvin Marketing is planning to kick off that new product introduction before the design is debugged or for Sally Sales to learn from Pete Production that the brand she loves to sell is having cost problems in production or from Al Accounting that it is producing zero profit margin.

Progress reports are a vital element of the management by contract process. There is no better discipline for improving MBO. They are a goals-oriented record of accomplishment against approved plans, a record of output of each of the processes that constitute, in the aggregate, operation of the enterprise. Progress reports are the vital link between objectives and the new higher performance standards that result from the process.

Every manager who prepares a plan should submit progress reports, using the plan as a baseline against which to report progress. It is the mechanism by which the plan is kept alive and up to date. A plan is effective and productive only when it is used in this way; otherwise it represents an annual ritual that produces paper but little else. And, unless the plan is used, it will quickly find its way from the desk top into a drawer or filing cabinet.

There is no practical reason why progress reporting cannot be pushed down the line to lower levels of management. There is no better management training, no better way to emphasize that results are more important than activity, and no better way to find out who has the potential for a higher management position.

OUTPUT AND RETURN ON INVESTMENT

Progress reports must be concerned with output, not with input or activity. Output is what moves the enterprise forward. The output of each transaction becomes the driving input to the succeeding transaction, the output of which becomes in turn input to the next, and so on. When the output of one transaction fails, it breaks the chain and reduces the productivity not simply of the following transaction but of all succeeding ones.

As an example, if a single sales representative in the field fails to follow through with paperwork after closing a sale (as often happens), it can have an adverse effect on the company's profitability and return on investment. *This effect may be barely perceptible, but it is nonetheless very real.* Here's how the process works. The incomplete customer order forms can hold up order processing until the missing information can be obtained. Delay at this juncture results in delaying the shop order or warehouse order, with its consequent delay in production and/or shipping. Delay in billing can result in later collection of the accounts receivable which adversely affects cash flow. The receivable, however small, inflates the total company investment, a factor of the return-on-investment equation, thus reducing turnover and percent return on operating investment. The adverse effects of such lapses, seemingly remote and inconsequential, are tangible, and the cumulative effect of many lapses can be devastating to productivity in the near term and to profitability in the long run.

Reports that are concerned with input or activity instead of output can also have a depressing effect on productivity. There are functional managers who are more interested in conserving resources than in utilizing them gainfully, often in the mistaken notion that they are serving the best interests of the firm. An example taken from life is the sales manager with the soul of a bookkeeper who is so concerned about the high-living habits of field sales representatives that their performance is judged by the size of their expense reports instead of their sales volume.

Activity-focused managers measure performance in terms of long hours worked, vacations not taken, meetings attended, or reports written. Their reports are self-centered "activity reports" not objectives-oriented progress reports and are of little use to the other managers whose own output is dependent on these managers' input to them.

Constant effort is required to keep the progress reporting focused on output. Even line managers whose output is very specific and measurable—units, tons, new order bookings, engineering drawings, or invoices—will often backslide into reporting input problems or activities. Most staff and knowledge workers tend to resist quantifying their output. Technical managers will claim that their output cannot be quantified, that hours of engineering effort are the only measure of their effectiveness. On an engineering project, progress will normally be reported as "percent completed," usually measured by number of hours and dollars expended related to the total hours and dollars in the estimate. These are measures of activity, of course, so cannot be accepted.

Scientists, lawyers, and other professionals in management have always been a particularly vexing problem in this respect. Robert Noyce, chief executive of Intel Corporation, a high-technology electronics company—and a scientist-manager himself—has found that this needn't be so, however. He requires progress reports from all of his top-level people and measures them in every aspect of their performance. His claim that "they love to be measured'" seems to be substantiated by the firm's technological leadership, rapid growth, and impressive financial performance.

In this connection, it is not uncommon for large firms to require from each manager a monthly activities report or status report covering in summary fashion all activities during the period. By emphasizing *activity* or *status*, reports of this type contribute to the problem; instead of focusing on results, managers tend to fill the required number of pages with details of their activities or statements of where they stand. Many of these reports read like this:

1. Met with engineering and product design to discuss quality problems on Model 510B.
2. Continued work on market survey of improved sump pump.
3. Sent for specifications and design information on new soft gasket.

Or worse, the reports confuse time expended with results:

1. Spent two days on variance analysis of May operating results.
2. Attended 5-day seminar on absorption costing.
3. Added two clerks to accounts payable staff.

These reports tell almost nothing except that the writer is busy. A shift of emphasis to results rather than activities, however, coupled with a change of report title can often work wonders. These progress reports now can provide real information.

1. Quality control problem on Model 510B resolved by changing design tolerances. Sales Department notified that revised specification sheet will be available by 7/31.
2. Preliminary results of sump pump market survey published 6/20. Indications are that new design will be accepted by distributors. Recommend proceed with pilot test in August.
3. Variance analysis of May results shows excessive scrap (125K), and indirect labor (75k), offset by a favorable purchase-price factor of 28K. Corrective action has been taken.

This type of report is information-rich, and reflects a strong objectives- and results-orientation. It is not as easy for managers to write, of course, because it requires deeper thought, more effort, and better organization of information. It also requires managers to stick out their necks a little further by making firm recommendations. A useful precondition for reporting of this kind is wide dissemination of company, division, and departmental objectives; as this discussion points out, active and intensive involvement is even better for the development of these objectives on the part of all managers.

SELF-CONTROL THROUGH PROGRESS REPORTING

It is in the area of performance review and appraisal that the self-control element of Drucker's "management by objectives and self-control" can be most effectively exercised. Most MBO programs rightly emphasize the value of participation in setting objectives; most recommend joint manager and boss reviews of performance, usually, however, on the boss's initiative and necessarily conducted within the context of a superior/subordinate relationship. Self-control by the manager can relieve this situation of the tensions and perceived threats by depersonalizing the feedback on performance.

In this concept, as developed by McGregor, managers appraise their own accomplishments periodically, based on feedback from control reports and records. The self-appraisals are then discussed with their superiors, after which new short-term performance goals are established. This shift of initiative alters the subordinate/superior relationship profoundly and redefines the superior's role from "that of a judge to that of a helper." The self-appraisal, moreover, gives the manager better insight and changes the emphasis "from an appraisal to identify weaknesses to an analysis of performance to define strengths and potential."[1]

MBO programs can falter from lack of sufficient and timely feedback on performance. Often this is a consequence of time pressures on superiors, which may prevent them from meeting with subordinate managers frequently enough or for a sufficient length of time to adequately review the performance of each. Carroll and Tosi cite research[2] proving quite conclusively that feedback improves performance and that the more specific, relevant, and timely the feedback is, the greater the positive effect it has on performance. They point out, however, that feedback must be used as a means of comparing performance with some previously established goals or standards. The self-appraisal concept forces managers to set up the control reports needed to measure their own progress toward goals; instead of passively awaiting the judgment of the boss on their performance, they can initiate action, facts in hand. If circumstances or schedule conflicts prevent a discussion, managers may lack the boss's *opinion*, but they won't be handicapped by lack of performance feedback on which to base operating decisions in the interim.

This goes to the heart of the debate about who should receive information on the individual manager's performance—the manager, the superior, or both. In the concept of self-control, the superior should be concerned primarily with progress toward long-term objectives, not with interim efforts or results. When managers monitor their own performance, they alone need to receive the current control data because they make the control decisions themselves. The superior's main concern is whether the control data is valid, unbiased, and utilized; he or she need not see it concurrently to make this judgment.

It is in this respect that many MBO programs doom themselves to failure. Feedback on performance to plan is essential to control of any process, of course, but true self-control requires that managers be permitted to adjust performance on the basis of their *own appraisals* of feedback information, not the boss's. This requires, in turn, that feedback be obtained from the process directly, not by way of the boss. When the manager's superior alone receives the feedback report or receives it first, he or she is in a position to exercise what George Carvalho has called "voodoo control" over the manager—a kind of control that is deadly to productivity.

The frequency of self-review needed by the manager is a function of the complexity, duration, and importance of the task being reviewed. It is not inconceivable that this could be daily. The frequency of *joint performance reviews* needed will vary with the number of objectives and associated tasks, the degree of difficulty of the goals, the number of discrete milestones or go/no-go decision points in each project, the confidence the superior has in the subordinate, and the leadership style of the boss. Weekly intervals are not uncommon, monthly reviews are more usual, and it is probably risky to go longer than a quarter without a thorough review.

It was pointed out earlier that it is essential to focus efforts toward achievement of a few difficult and demanding objectives rather than to strive toward a great many less challenging goals. In every operation, there are a critical few activities that make the real difference between outstanding results and ordinary performance, between success and mediocrity, and between market dominance and mere participation in the market. It is essential to identify these and to set objectives that will focus the intelligence and capabilities of the organization on those that count most.

The research cited by Carroll and Tosi has demonstrated that the act of setting goals has a measurable effect on performance and that more demanding goals result in improved performance. Further, more difficult objectives appear to increase performance consistently. Individuals tend to set performance goals higher than previous performance levels and tend to keep them higher; levels of aspiration seem to be a function of prior success or failure. They observe that hard, specific goals are more motivational than vague goals, however inspirational the latter may be.

PERFORMANCE APPRAISAL AND COMPENSATION

In most MBO programs, performance appraisals typically are conducted quarterly or semiannually, at which time manager and superior discuss progress toward the objectives, reasons for nonperformance, outlook for the near future, potential for development, and establishment of new objectives for the next performance period. The basis for the discussion is usually a performance appraisal report submitted by the manager. Frequently, the review is tied in to an appraisal of the manager's job performance, attitudes, and relations with others, at which time some of the objectivity tends to be lost. In too many cases, discussion involves the sensitive matter of compensation and can become totally subjective, both participants losing sight of the real purpose of MBO—which is to achieve goals that move the company forward while permitting managers to fully develop their own potential for personal growth.

Almost no one questions the desirability of linking MBO with the organization's monetary reward system, but the application of this principle in practice may well be one of the most difficult tasks of management. In Babcock and Sorensen's "Long Range Approach to Management by Objectives," the integration of MBO with the compensation system doesn't take place until the final stage of implementation. This critical and sensitive phase of MBO should be preceded, in their view, by 2 to 5 years of preparation, training, and psychological conditioning of the organization.[3]

It is important to keep a clear distinction between performance appraisal for compensation purposes and review of performance for purposes of improving the manager's chances of achieving objectives.

The former frequently is influenced by factors extraneous to the manager's performance, in particular the constraints imposed by a formal management salary plan and departmental expense budgets, not to mention current company profitability. Salary reviews all too often emphasize personality, attitudes, and past behavior rather than performance and future actions.

There is considerable difference of opinion on this issue, to be sure, but Douglas Sherwin makes the point that many of the most important objectives of an organization cannot be achieved through a single person's efforts, therefore the individual's performance cannot be measured against these. He states, "Performance appraisals are indispensable, but they cannot logically be based upon the results of the MBO objectives alone."[4] William Mobley, while favoring a close linkage between MBO and merit compensation, concedes that it may tend to skew the efforts of managers toward the more measurable aspects of the job at the expense of other important, though more subjective, performance factors.[5]

It may well be more productive for the bosses to confine themselves to performance reviews focused on objectives and progress toward them and to stay out of the compensation bargaining process altogether. The annual salary review can be conducted by an agent, typically someone from the personnel or wage and salary group, who can conduct the review on a less personal basis, within the context of a structured salary plan and annual merit increase budgets. This is not to say that compensation can be separated from performance, only that salary negotiations should be kept separate from the performance review for MBO purposes.

The practice of awarding regular salary increases based upon achievement of objectives may even be counterproductive in the long run. It may lead to a situation in which a manager with a good performance record becomes overpaid in relation both to the job function and to peer managers. Some degree of motivation may be lost when this happens, and there is almost no way compensation can be adjusted downward in the event performance during a subsequent period falters. It is better to keep base salary tied to the position description—to responsibility and authority—and to reward exceptional performance with a money bonus that can be withheld when performance comes up short.

NOTES

[1] McGregor, Douglas, "An Uneasy Look At Performance Appraisal," *Harvard Business Review*, September/October 1972.

[2] Carroll, Steven J., Jr., and Tosi, Henry L., *MBO: Applications and Research*, The Macmillan Company, New York, 1973.

[3] Babcock, Richard, and Sorensen, P.F., "A Long Range Approach to MBO," *Management Review*, July 1976. (New York: AMACOM, a division of American Management Associations.)

[4]. Sherwin, Douglas, " Management of Objectives," *Harvard Business Review*, May/June 1976.

[5] Mobley, William, "The Link Between MBO and Merit Compensation," *Personnel Journal*, June 1974.

HOW TO CLOSE
THE OBJECTIVES GAP

NEW PERFORMANCE STANDARDS—
STEP 10 OF THE PROCESS

It was observed earlier that the objectives of the truly productive enterprise are never fully accomplished, because they are constantly being raised higher. In ITT during Harold Geneen's management, for instance, whenever a subsidiary company, a division, or a staff function appeared to be in a position to meet its business plan goals, Geneen would usually arrange to set some new targets that would stretch the capabilities of the unit's management further. In Western Union, during its transition from an old-line telegraph company to a modern electronic telecommunications services organization, management followed a practice known as the "sack of sand" philosophy. Whenever it appeared that a manager could carry a load easily, the boss would pile on another sack of sand in the form of added responsibility or more challenging goals.

This final phase of the management by contract process is the task of anchoring the gains you have made through the preceding nine steps. This is accomplished by documenting at the end of the period (normally year-end) the new, higher performance standards you have reached; and by recording in summary form the progress you have made toward your objectives. The mechanism for doing this is your monthly progress reports, which constitute a running record of your interim gains as you implemented your improvement plans.

It cannot be emphasized too strongly or repeated often enough that management by contract is a process. The process was described in an early chapter. It may be helpful at this point to recapitulate the whole process in terms of a summary review of the steps you have gone through and how each of them built on the prior steps. Following this brief recapitulation, the output of the entire process will be summed up.

**CHAPTER
FIFTEEN**

RECAP OF THE TEN-STEP PROCESS

- Step 1 built a foundation of facts by identifying your functional strengths and weaknesses and isolating the most critical of these for concentrated management attention.
- Step 2 created the challenge by setting demanding objectives to improve those critical factors and, in so doing, enhanced your contribution to the forward progress of the enterprise.
- Step 3 translated these goals into actions by defining specific plans to achieve your objectives (and, at the same time, reconciling these to the needs and capabilities of your subordinates).
- Step 4 created a degree of coordination with other managers through a process of mutual reconciliation of goals and plans with your colleagues.
- Step 5 helped you get your share of resources through negotiations with your superior, during which you undoubtedly modified your goals and plans to bring them into accord with your supervisor's— and the company's—needs, norms, and values. (At this point, as well, you reconciled any unresolved disputes with your peers.)
- Step 6 documented the agreement with your superior, the understanding you have jointly reached as to your respective roles and relationships as you work together toward achievement of the goals and plans you have agreed on.
- Step 7 was a process of implementing your plans through self-management, guided by the contractual document, and of controlling your own progress through feedback reports on actual performance.
- Step 8 established a mechanism for coping with change and turbulence, using control reports on internal events and external developments to adapt your plans to new circumstances.
- Step 9 provided a medium, progress reports, to ensure that you get credit for your gains (and also to flag problems and opportunities to the attention of higher management).

The output of the final step—closing the objectives gap—becomes *input* to the annual recycling of the total process, which begins each time from a new and higher plateau of functional performance. The new performance standards also represent benchmarks for the organization to maintain while the improvement process is repeated.

The feedback loop is completed at this point, as the new performance standards of the function are incorporated into the next functional self-appraisal. Depending on the condition of the firm when the management by contract program is instituted, it may take a number of iterations before the overall goals of the organization are approached. Each iteration takes the enterprise closer. But the gap is never fully closed, it can only be narrowed.

OUTPUT OF THE TOTAL PROCESS

The output of the total process is highly productive performance of its assigned mission by each function—performance that is enhanced by closer and more effective coordination among functions. In quantitative terms, this can result in increased product output, improved product quality, accelerated cash flow, higher asset turnover, and increased return on investment. For participating managers, the output of the process can be enhanced work satisfaction, a heightened sense of shared mission, and a greater degree of self-actualization.

THE LARGER PURPOSE OF MANAGEMENT BY CONTRACT

Management by contract has implications that go far beyond the functional or operating level of organization. The process can provide essential input to the executive level where corporate policy is formulated, strategic plans developed, organizations structured and restructured, and resources allocated. The process has value in organizations that are experiencing difficulty; its greater value, however, may be in companies that are growing and in apparent good health. There, it serves as a structured process of continuous profit improvement. These broader implications are discussed in a context of actual situations as well as in theory.

PART FOUR

MANAGEMENT BY CONTRACT IN ACTION

THE ITT MANAGEMENT PROCESS

Wherever the fundamentals that underlie the management by contract process have been effectively applied, the results have been gratifying in terms of enhanced managerial productivity. Within my own experience, these principles have been applied to good effect in situations as varied as a large multinational conglomerate, a sizable communications services organization, a high-volume container manufacturer, a large producer of building products, a small advertising agency, and a start-up operation in the energy conservation field.

In organizations where the MBO process is regarded as a mutual agreement between manager and boss to work toward specified goals rather than as a time-consuming paper chase, the goals that are set tend to be more demanding, and performance toward their accomplishment tends to be more effective.

The integrated business planning process used by Harold Geneen to manage the huge worldwide conglomerate corporation known as ITT is a highly developed form of management by objectives and self-control. In several important aspects, it approaches the management by contract process presented in this book. As a matter of fact, the process described here brings together and integrates with the business planning several management control systems that were developed and used separately in ITT during the period of its greatest development.

In the ITT process, each one of the more than 200 operating units, ranging in size from a couple of million to a couple of billion dollars in assets and serving such diverse markets as aerospace, home building, automotive, telecommunications, personal finance, insurance, food, and many, many others, prepares an annual business plan of surpassing thoroughness. Each plan document contains (for each product

CHAPTER SIXTEEN

line of significance and for each supporting function) objectives, improvement plans, and detailed financial projections for the following year and the subsequent 4 years. Data for the first year are in detail by month and quarter; data for subsequent years are less detailed.

Objectives for product lines and functional departments are based upon clear assumptions, critical analysis, and hard information (Geneen's passion for "unshakable facts" is legendary). Improvement plans contain all five essential plan elements—firm assignment of responsibility, target completion dates, identification of needed resources, estimates of costs, and estimates of benefits.

A form of "peer review" is built into the process to ensure that each manager knows what peer managers are staking out as their business missions and areas of responsibility and to ensure that each is aware of what others are proposing to do during the plan period. Additionally, a series of review meetings with department heads is held in order to minimize overlapping and duplication of effort.

Each ITT business plan undergoes a rigorous battery of testing, cross-examinations, and review as it takes final form. Beyond any doubt, the final plan represents firm commitment to objectives by product-line and functional managers. Approval of the plan by their organizational superiors represents equal commitment on their part to provide the resources identified in the plan.

The formal business plan review at ITT world headquarters or ITT Europe headquarters is more than a ceremonial endorsement of these plans. It represents a highly visible commitment by the chief executive to provide resources and support to the unit manager whose plans and objectives meet with corporate approval. Needless to say, the knowledge that product-line and functional objectives will be exposed to the CEO and the top executive staff has a pronounced beneficial effect on managers all the way down the line. Objectives must stretch capabilities or they won't be accepted; they must be realistic or they won't stand up under the review process.

The process represents a thoughtful combination of two basic approaches to planning: one, a technical approach that builds upon a solid set of facts to create a rational projection of future performance; and two, a motivational approach that acts to enhance current performance and future development of managers.

To my mind, deeply involved as I was in the development and the implementation of the ITT business planning process, there is little doubt that these plans constitute a form of MBO contract between managers and their organizational superiors. I believe this to be the view, as well, of Gerry Andlinger and Hanford Willard, the two principal architects of the system.

Apart from the formal business planning process, but related to it, are a number of highly developed ITT management control systems. Some are closely integrated into the planning system; some are independent of it. In the first category is the budgeting system, which uses as its initial input the financial projections for the first year, and a highly structured system for reporting progress against the first year's improvement plans.

An external control report, dubbed a "monthly manager's letter" and submitted by each unit manager, reports events and developments throughout ITT's worldwide marketplace. These letters are disseminated to product-line managers and others who have a need to know what is going on throughout the world.

Early in the conversion of ITT from a holding company to a "managed" organization, Geneen instituted a monthly staff-effectiveness report in which all staff executives were directed to document "measurable results" for the period; results were defined as "dollar measured results of aid given to the line organization." This was intended, he said, "to put an end to business plans that do not become realities and earnings forecasts that evaporate each December." In this way, Geneen forced staff people to think and act in the same terms as line managers—profit, return on investment, and growth—not simply in terms of their narrow professional interests.

Quite apart from the planning process, a checklist system was developed in the late 1960s for making in-depth appraisals of functions in ITT operating units. The system was implemented worldwide and provided useful input to the planning process but was never integrated into it. The principles underlying this system have been applied to the ten point self-appraisal, which forms the bedrock foundation for objective setting in the management by contract process.

The sum total of these several ITT programs is a management control system that has few equals in the corporate world. Kirby Warren, head of the management department of Columbia University's Business School, was recently quoted as saying, "I've been looking at corporate planning and control systems for 20 years and I've seen none better than ITT's under Geneen."*

Does management by objectives as an implied contract work? ITT is a compelling case for the affirmative. The company doubled its net income every 5 years for more than 2 decades; sales and revenues increased correspondingly.

* *The New York Times*, Apr. 6, 1980.

Much of this growth resulted, to be sure, from a massive acquisition program, but without effective planning and control systems—and management by objectives as an operating philosophy—this incredible growth rate could never have been managed and sustained. There can be little doubt, as well, about its value as a personal development process to the managers who participated. Managers with ITT experience have become desirable targets for executive headhunters, and hundreds have moved on to become top executives of major corporations throughout the world. The process has benefited the other constituencies of the corporation, too. High productivity, superior product quality, and technological advances in many areas have benefited users of the firm's products and services. Sixteen consecutive years of profit gains and dividend increases benefited ITT's shareholders. And surely the hundreds of thousands of employees and retirees, thousands of suppliers, and the general public have gained from the firm's stability, growth, and diversification.

This is not in any way to imply that a system or a set of procedures alone can make a firm successful; without vision, flair, and wisdom in the front office, the finest planning and control systems in the world are only paper exercises.

(ITT's phenomenal success seems to contradict Peter Drucker's opinion that (a) a multinational company is difficult to manage, (b) a conglomerate company is difficult to manage, and (c) a multinational conglomerate is totally unmanageable and an abomination. Of course it will only be after several years have passed since Harold S. Geneen has stepped down that we will know whether ITT can be managed by mere mortals.)

THE ITT TALENT SPIN-OFF

The ITT planning and control processes have since become rather widely disseminated, as managers moved on from ITT to become chief executives, chief operating officers, and other top executives of large companies throughout the world, taking with them the principles learned during their attendance at the "Harold Geneen School for Advanced Management," as ITT was called by some, not entirely facetiously. One of these talented young managers was George Haufler, an ITT worldwide product-line manager for a time and later president of a sizable ITT group. Haufler left ITT in 1971 to take over the presidency of CertainTeed Products Corporation's fiberglass group. During the preceding years, this group had built up operating losses of $13 million. One of Haufler's first actions was to direct his managers to develop a 5-year business plan; he made his intentions emphatic and specific by prescribing ITT's type of integrated business planning to objectives and by setting a tight deadline for its completion.

Haufler was advised that it was quite unrealistic to impose a task of such comprehension and depth upon managers who had not been indoctrinated in planning and MBO. His personnel director contended that it would take at least 2 years to train and condition the management for such a task. Haufler took a firm stand on the issue, brought in an outside resource to help in structuring the plan and counseling the inexperienced, and succeeded in producing a credible plan, complete with department objectives, improvement plans, schedules, and financial projections. The plan called for a turnaround in the first year of the plan period; not only was the turnaround accomplished, but the group turned in net income of $10 million, substantially in excess of objectives.

The process succeeded also in shaking out a number of managers who could not adjust to a rigorous MBO approach to management, particularly when Haufler made it clear that he considered each plan to represent a contract to perform. Some transferred to other company groups where the pressures for results were less intense; a few left. Although in this instance this particular consequence was unexpected and certainly had not been premeditated, it was not entirely unwelcome. Thus it appears that an operation which is in deep trouble and burdened by deadwood in its management may well benefit from a tough contractual approach to management by objectives.

Haufler was later promoted to president of the CertainTeed Corporation, and expanded the MBO program to encompass all 12,000 employees. By 1976, the fiberglass operation—by then a separate operating group—was contributing to CertainTeed net income of $37 million a year on $200 million of sales, and the total corporation moved on to set new records for growth.

A PERSONAL CASE HISTORY

I was deeply involved in the development of ITT's integrated business planning process, control reporting, progress reporting, and operations auditing systems from 1959 to 1970—the period during which Harold Geneen converted a $750-million holding company into a multi-billion-dollar multinational management corporation through growth planning, tight controls, diversification, and acquisition. I was a member of the ITT world headquarters planning group during the early part of this period, when these programs were being conceived, developed, installed, and refined. During the second half of the decade, I had staff responsibility for implementing the business planning in a highly diversified $2 billion group of divisions and subsidiary companies—about fifty in number. The shift of roles, from one involving *development* of the program to one involving *implementation*, provided new insight into the process of management by objectives as a practical matter.

During this latter period, I also functioned as chairman of the North American Economic Advisory Council, which I organized to provide economic guidance to ITT top management about the business climate in the United States, Canada, and the Caribbean. In this capacity, I became more appreciative of the need to view the corporation and its external environment as an integral, interdependent unit.

ITT's acquisition machinery was in high gear during the 1960s. For several years I had the task of indoctrinating and training the top management of a number of these acquired companies in the ITT management and planning processes. Many of these organizations had been built by entrepreneurs from small ventures into sizable firms and had reached a stage where the owner's personal management style had become a liability; the kind of professional management that ITT was noted for was needed. A never-failing source of astonishment as well as personal gratification to me was the eagerness with which the subordinate managers in these companies accepted the ITT highly structured system of planning and controls. To many, it represented the first opportunity to participate meaningfully in the making of decisions that affected their futures and the *privilege* of being asked for their recommendations for improving effectiveness of their own operations. Also for many, the change from an autocratic command-centered form of management to management by objectives and a degree of self-control brought about a gratifying release of creativity that had obviously been pent up by the previous management environment.

I moved on from ITT to become a vice president of a communications company with operations throughout the United States. The firm is small compared to ITT—about $600 million in annual sales and revenues and about $1.5 billion of assets—but it is an important member of the communications industry. The company was at the time midway through a massive transition to a full-line telecommunications organization from its former single-product service character. This required nothing less than the total modernization of its physical plant, the upgrading of its technical capabilities, and the building of a brand-new sales force. At the same time, the company was phasing out the obsolete facilities and reducing the large payroll it took to operate and maintain them.

The problem had been likened by the CEO to "turning an elephant around in a bathtub." It was complicated greatly by the constraints of government regulation and a union contract in which management had given up many of its prerogatives to manage.

The new assignment involved general management and profit responsibility for all of the firm's operations in seven northeastern states, which employed about 800 people and produced some $30 million of annual revenues from a mix of old and new services. This area had a unique set of problems of its own, in addition to those of the total organization. It ranked among the lowest in the company performance measurements for profitability and growth, the internal organization was in disarray, and morale was at a disastrously low level. People had no firm objectives; they appeared to lurch from crisis to crisis. Controls were virtually nonexistent. Expenses were running at very high levels as a result of some programs that had been adopted without adequate planning or preparation.

The six managers who reported directly to the area vice president were barely on speaking terms. Prior area management had created a corrosive atmosphere of distrust among people through authoritarian management, closed-door meetings, and almost total lack of communication to the point where information had just about ceased to flow between managers in different functions. In short, the operation showed all the classic symptoms of a business in deep distress.

It did not appear to be a "people" problem. The managers and supervisors in place were experienced and apparently competent; they were simply overwhelmed by events. Yesterday's failures were totally consuming today's energies; small problems were growing into large problems for lack of attention; and managers had no time left to deal with opportunities that would sustain the business in the future. Replacing people could only aggravate an already critical situation.

The pressing task was to help these managers get a handle on their immediate problems, to help them catalog their difficulties and set up a plan to contain them while permanent solutions were worked out. Clearly, there were no quick fixes possible; no dramatic actions could resolve these serious issues rapidly. Only a time-phased program of remedial action could repair the damages and prevent recurrence, and that was a serious job of work.

As the program progressed, the managers were pleased to find that the crises that had been consuming their time and energy could be progressively resolved over a period of months; and as each situation became less critical, its demands on their time and resources diminished. Thus, as current problems were gradually put behind them, their physical and human resources could be put to more productive uses. The next step was to identify potential problems *before* they happened—to find and defuse any land mines that might be buried in the path ahead. This created a second order of priority claim on available resources during the coming months. Only after these two steps were completed could managers set goals and allocate resources to go after new opportunities.

These tasks were not easy ones for individuals who had been functioning in a crisis environment for a long time. Clearly, they were not accustomed to looking ahead much further than next week, rarely to next month. During the first few months, many hours of discussion were needed to define problems and decide on the proper action to take. It was a productive exercise, however, because out of the free and open discussions came a sense of unity of purpose and a new spirit of cooperation among managers who heretofore had worked in tight functional compartments. Managers took to it eagerly and responded with gratifying enthusiasm.

The output of the process was, for each manager, a documented set of well-defined goals based on the hard realities of the situation, a set of action plans that represented genuine commitment, and identification of the resources and support needed to make it all happen. On the part of the area vice president, we agreed, the responsibility was to provide funding and facilities and to help by knocking down the administrative roadblocks that corporate bureaucracy tends to erect in the way of people who actively seek to put the company's resources to new uses. Accordingly, the program took on the nature of an agreement between each manager and the area vice president— a contract in effect if not in documented form—to work together toward the negotiated goals.

Because of the area's relative remoteness from the corporate headquarters, the area vice president also had an obligation to keep managers informed about changes in company policies, long-range objectives, strategies, and organization (to the extent that the latter two were not sensitive) that could have an effect on their objectives and plans. In my experience, the conventional channels of commution for such information are often inadequate. This required frequent and often lengthy staff meetings in which the implications of the changes were assessed by the group and action was assigned when called for. The benefits of this process in building a group spirit far outweighed the management time spent in the meetings.

Only after managers showed evidence that they had firm control over their operations and their problems were the other elements of the management by contract process adopted. Only then was the oral contract formalized into a document containing the manager's statement of objectives, a detailed improvement plan, and a listing of resources required. Going into the second year, the program was moved down to the second level of management. Each individual reporting to an area manager was expected to set objectives, prepare improvement plans, and share these with fellow managers and supervisors (later these were formalized into contracts in the same form). Each area manager now had two contractual relationships to honor: one with subordinates, to provide them with the resources and support needed to achieve their goals and plans; the other with his or her organizational superior, to carry out the plans and work sincerely toward the goals on which they both had agreed.

It must be said that several of the older managers found it difficult to adjust to the new and rigorous mode of operation. They either transferred to other areas or opted to take advantage of a generous company early-retirement plan. Several others needed a good deal of coaching and encouragement before they could adapt. Another problem that surfaced early was the tendency for some managers to overpromise, to overreach in setting their objectives, in their eagerness to please the new boss. It is important to correct this in order to avoid the sting of failure later.

The results of the program were gratifying—and impressive. Within 30 months, the area had moved up to the top ranks in the company performance measurements, becoming number one in the heavily weighted financial and operating measurements and nearing the top in sales and technical services. Despite an obsolete product line that was losing volume at a rate of 15 percent a year, total revenues were up by 17.5 percent as new services more than took up the slack. The operating margin—a key measure of profitability—was up by 27 percent, while the ratio of operating margin to revenues increased to 51.7 percent from 43.3 percent 2 years earlier. Expenses had been reduced by $1 million a year through employee attrition and closing of unproductive facilities. As a consequence of these actions, productivity as measured by operating margin per employee increased a startling 53.5 percent, from $14,481 to $22,257.

The company performance measurements did not include return on assets, but an informal calculation in the area showed a better than 60 percent improvement in this important ratio, resulting from the increased return on revenues together with a reduction in accounts receivables and disposal of obsolete facilities. (Inventories are not a large investment factor in a service business of this kind.)

THE MOTIVATIVE VALUE OF SUCCESS

There's more to the story than is shown by the numbers. Buoyed by success in meeting early objectives, area management tackled a number of more audacious projects. In the marketing arena, Ma Bell was taken on in her most sensitive market, long-distance voice transmission, which area management now offered to business customers at rates below AT&T. Others have since moved into this lucrative market, among them RCA and ITT, but there was great satisfaction in being the David who first took on the communications Goliath. In a company that was traditionally WASP and in a geographic area not particularly hospitable to minorities, the area fielded a sales force that was more than 20 percent black and headed by a black area sales manager (the highest ranking minority employee in the whole company). The area equal employment opportunity affirmative action program, headed by a woman, was among the top performers in the company.

The high barriers between management and labor were broken down with the formation of an informal advisory board of employees; this was the first time that nonmanagement people were brought into the area decision-making process. This board met monthly for a full day to discuss problems at the operating level, and its input was exceedingly valuable to area management. The union vice president, initially hostile to the idea, dropped his opposition after attending a couple of sessions.

During the period, more than a dozen people were promoted to positions of higher responsibility within the area, including three women and three so-called minorities. The area gained a reputation (and a measure of influence at headquarters) by having four of its managers recruited for important staff jobs at corporate. Two others moved to higher-level positions in other areas. All this upward mobility was highly visible, of course, and decidedly encouraging as well to managers who had been frozen into their positions for years.

Some home office executives, however, regarded the activity with suspicion. The idea of promoting an individual into a higher-level job before he or she was qualified beyond any doubt was considered risky, if not downright foolish. Yet our experience showed that it was more productive to fill an open position with a person somewhat less than fully ready for it. The individual was forced to stretch his or her capabilities, and in the process both the person and the job benefited. The person who was qualified beyond any doubt could do the job better, to be sure, but only initially; when there was no challenge to surpass his or her previous capabilities, the individual tended to give the job less than 100 percent. The less-qualified person needed more guidance and support, naturally, as well as a large measure of encouragement and understanding. But in the long run, it was found, everyone gained; the individual gained in management skill and confidence, the person's boss gained insight into the job and capability in dealing with subordinates, and the organization gained a more competent, self-assured manager.

Mistakes were made, of course, but their effects were minimal compared to the benefits. The process itself has an inherent capability to detect a wrong course of action or an incompetent manager long before irremediable damage is done. A second lesson was learned, as well—the small mistakes that subordinate managers may make when they are delegated genuine authority are less damaging and less costly than the gross mistakes that can result from highly centralized authority. As an example, one of the area's most troublesome problems—one which took 2 years to resolve—was the consequence of a front-office decision that had been made without consulting the managers involved.

The principal lesson of this experience is that the organization cannot be made more productive through threat of punishment, executive exhortation to work harder for the good of the company, or even financial reward for greater output. The organization can become more productive only by tapping the potential that resides in each person and directing it toward objectives that he or she will find fulfilling. The financial rewards are important, of course, not only for their own value, but as evidence that the individual's contribution is being recognized and appreciated.

A LESSON OF FAILURE

A more recent experience with the process in a sizable manufacturing corporation may be enlightening. It emphatically points up that no management program, regardless of how effective, can succeed without executive-office support.

The company is fairly large—about $600 million of sales and $1 billion of assets. It markets a broad line of products to the construction industry. Plants, warehouses, and sales offices are located throughout the United States. The program was initiated by the president and chief operating officer of the firm, who had observed some serious inefficiencies in production facilities during his periodic visits. He was also concerned about the effectiveness of several headquarters functional groups. He had already installed programs for strategic long-range planning and for operational planning but sensed a need for short-term improvement planning throughout the staff as well as the line organization.

Building upon prior development work with the system, I spent some time tailoring the process to the unique characteristics of the organization. The program was presented to a meeting of the executive staff and was approved for implementation. It was apparent that the cordial reception the program received was due as much to its origin in the president's office as to its own merits, of course, and that the real acceptance would come only from success in operation. With this in mind, it was decided to implement it on a phased basis, starting with a single staff department and one production operation.

It seems almost mandatory that a new management program have an acronym—this one became the AIM Program, from the initials of the Appraisal and Improvement Matrix, as the form was then entitled. Initially, there was no attempt to sell the program as management by contract—this was to come at a later stage, after an extensive period of conditioning and application. The program was perceived as a long-range one, with full implementation to be measured in years rather than months.

To ensure success, it was first implemented in a corporate staff department—advertising and promotion—whose manager had been involved in the design and who was most enthusiastic about its potential for improving the effectiveness of her function. She used the checklists extensively and found a number of unsuspected shortcomings and deficiencies in her operation which she was able to correct over a period of time.

Most significantly, she discovered a disturbing preoccupation with form rather than substance in the firm's print advertising—a concern with *design* directed more toward winning graphic-association awards and the admiration of associates than toward generating inquiries for the sales department. Image or institutional themes dominated, often obscuring the product benefits story.

The process resulted in a set of objectives for each of her direct reports that redirected most of the advertising budget to the product message and the generation of solid leads for the sales department. Managers who prided themselves on their creativity found to their surprise that this kind of results-oriented advertising was even more demanding on their creative talents than the previous kind (after an initial shock of being measured on a "cost per lead" basis).

Feedback from this experience also resulted in a redesign of the matrix to tie it more closely to the checklists—a significant improvement that is incorporated in the Objectives and Improvement Matrix described in this book.

During this period of staff implementation, the program was also introduced in a production operation whose manager had a reputation for innovation and experimentation. He had recently taken over the operation and found it to be in serious trouble, lacking quality control and financial controls and shot through with deep-seated morale problems. The AIM Program was introduced in a series of brief meetings with the manager and his staff. It quickly became apparent that some conditioning and indoctrination would be needed before the program could become effective. Accordingly, a trial period of several months was scheduled during which each manager was individually coached. Periodic operating crises flared up, providing serious distraction from the AIM Program, but headway *was* being made, and managers became increasingly more supportive as they saw the results.

Before the division could move on to Step 2 of the process, the president and chief operating officer found himself at odds with the chairman and CEO on a couple of major policy issues—principally involving the purchase of a majority interest in the firm by European interests. He lost the battle—and his job. Within the next few months, most of the planning and control programs he had introduced were either dismantled or stripped of authority.

One of the casualties was the AIM Program. Never really terminated, the program died from neglect. Without the motivative power of top-level support, it survived only in the advertising department and barely clung to life in the operating division. The chances of reviving and expanding the program are slim, despite the departure of the chairman less than a year after he fired the president.

Not so incidentally, the company's operating results are down, its financial condition has deteriorated, and its common share price dropped nearly 50 percent in the year following the dismissal of the president.

THE BOTTOM LINE

PRODUCTIVITY AND PROFIT

The value of any management process must be measured, in the final analysis, by the tangible benefits it provides to the productivity and profitability of the enterprise. Profitability is virtually a direct function of productivity—which is, in turn, a derivative of the applied energy and intelligence of people. A management process that has the capability to evoke and stimulate the latent potential of people to put forth their best efforts as individuals and as members of work groups—even though these efforts are only fractionally better than before—can have beneficial effects on profitability that are quite remarkable. With payrolls running at a rather typical eight times net profit, a broad-based improvement of only 5 percent in people's productivity can quickly translate into a 40 percent increase in the firm's bottom line.

Profit, in its simplest terms, is a by-product of a job well done, says John Canas, CEO of the fast-growing Dunfey Hotel Corporation and the man responsible for the productivity of all Dunfey employees. He goes on to say that, when you really believe this, it triggers a process and, if you do it well, you'll make money. Operating hotels is the ultimate service business, of course, but the process is equally if not more important to businesses less closely coupled to the consumer.

CONVENTIONAL APPROACHES TO PROFIT IMPROVEMENT

Some years ago, J. Roger Morrison and Richard F. Neuschel discussed alternative management processes as approaches to profit improvement, designed to cope with the long-term decline in profitability of industry. They identified three basic approaches: (1) cost reduction by decree, (2) analytical review of operations, and (3) search for fundamental change; and they analyzed each in terms of its stimulus, the scope of action taken, time required for results,

CHAPTER SEVENTEEN

roles of management, and key requirements for effective implementation. Their bias was clearly toward the third approach, of course, as the one with the most enduring results, but they recognized that the other approaches may be called for in times of financial distress.

Their conclusions were summarized in Table 17.1, reproduced by permission of the *Harvard Business Review*.[1]

TABLE 17-1 Three Approaches to Profit Improvement

	I *Cost Reduction* *by Decree*	*II* *Analytical Review* *of Operations*	*III* *Search for* *Fundamental Change*
1. Typical stimulus	Financial crisis	Downturn in rate of growth, sales, or profit	Changing environment, aggressive philosophy of management
2. Approach	Executive order to cut costs by arbitrary amount	Careful search for higher yield and/or lower costs in existing functions	Broad study of basic policies, organization, facilities, and profit potential of company and its businesses
3. Scope of resulting action	Cost reduction only	Improvement in the way activities are carried out as well as in supervisory profit-orientation and analytical skill	Major changes in basic policies, structure, and facilities; elimination of unprofitable businesses, facilities, and activities
4. Time required for results	Immediate impact	May require months or years for complete review	Varies, but implementation of major change is usually slow
5. Character of actual results	Early results can be substantial but rarely lasting	Permanent results can accumulate to a very large and clearly provable profit increment	May yield largest, most dramatic long-term profit increment, but sometimes more difficult to measure precisely
6. Key roles	Chief executive who issues and enforces directive	Top management, which initiates study; middle management, which carries out resulting programs	Chief executive and staff, who develop basic alternatives
7. Key requirement	Discipline—to carry out decree	Training—to put improvement into effect	Imagination—to conceive new arrangements

DANGERS OF "RADICAL SURGERY"
COST CUTTING

The first approach—arbitrary cost reduction—can have serious adverse effects, the authors pointed out. This approach can damage some functions severely in the short run if it results in actions that cut organizational muscle and tissue along with accumulated fat. Across-the-board cost reduction so obviously penalizes and demotivates the efficient manager who runs a tight ship as to hardly need comment. What is worse, bloodletting budget cuts in already anemic operations seldom correct the basic weakness that caused the high costs in the first place.

It should be pointed out, too, that there is often a significant time lag between the issuance of a cost reduction decree from the executive office and its impact on the bottom line. In the Chrysler situation, for instance, the effects of massive cutbacks in the salaried work force and the shutdown of a dozen facilities during 1979 and 1980 took much longer than anticipated—more than 6 months—to show up as savings. Conceivably, a company could be in a period of rising market demand by the time that cuts in personnel and facilities take effect and thus be unable to respond with increased output.

Just as a surgeon's choices of procedure may be limited by a patient's critical condition, however, this method may be one of the few options open to the management of an operation in financial crisis.

PROFIT MAXIMIZING

The second approach—cost reduction through analytical review of operations—is clearly superior to the first. Problems may arise, however, if the signals from the executive office are misread by managers as emphasizing the *maximizing of profit* to the exclusion of other factors. In an organization that is experiencing unfavorable trends in revenues, net income, or share of market, the pressures upon managers to stop the downturn and improve profit margins rapidly can be irresistible. These pressures can lead to actions that do, in fact, have an immediate beneficial impact on net income—but at a high cost to the future of the business. Reduced reinvestment of earnings in R&D, quality assurance, and customer service is an easy way to increase the bottom line. Easy, that is, until competition moves into the firm's markets with better products, or product recalls cost months of production, or customers turn to others because their unhappiness with their purchases is unrecognized.

THE ISSUE IS THE SEARCH

The third approach was presented as a kind of "ultimate solution" to improved profitability. It has this appearance, to be sure, but the appearance may be deceiving. There is no denying that a "search for fundamental change" is a necessary factor in the major redirection of a firm that has ceased to grow with its markets and appears to be out of joint with its environment. The issue it raises is how and by whom the search is conducted.

The fallacy in the concept may lie in its total top-down orientation. The difficulty in its implementation is in determining *which basic policies* are out-of-phase with the firm's various publics; *which organizational structure* needs redesign; *which facilities, businesses, and activities* are unproductive; and *which changes* will yield the most beneficial results.

A FOURTH APPROACH TO
PROFITABILITY IMPROVEMENT

These determinations cannot be made easily, nor can they be made on a one-time basis. The process of change is continuous and cannot be halted while a study is being made. Such a study may be obsoleted by events by the time it is published. What is needed, it seems, is a mechanism by which the highest decision level of the enterprise is provided, on a continuous basis and through a structured process, with guidance from the operating level of the organization.

This may appear to be a turnabout; the notion that the upper echelon needs guidance from the lower seems to violate the principles of organizational hierarchy. It is unwise to assume, however, that top management of an enterprise has the wisdom to develop and articulate such vital expressions of corporate intention as policies, objectives and strategies, delegations of authority, and organization designs, without a vigorous flow of guiding information from the operating and environment-sensing functions of the organization. This is particularly pertinent as the economy becomes more and more knowledge- and information-based. It is in this respect that the management by contract process serves a larger purpose than that of simply improving productivity of the operating organization, important as that may be. This greater function is illustrated by the addition of a column to the table designed by Morrison and Neuschel. Here the process is depicted as a fourth approach to profit improvement, "Adoption of a Structured Process of Continuous Improvement," and

TABLE 17.2

	Adoption of a Structured Process of Continuous Improvement
1. Typical stimulus	Uneasiness and uncertainty whether the enterprise is realizing its real and full potential; and a fear that profit, while seemingly high, may be inadequate to ensure survival.
2. Approach	Highly structured process of management based on self-appraisal, objective setting, improvement planning, and self-control by managers.
3. Scope of resulting action	Productivity (output) of each function is increased; effectiveness of interrelationships between functions is improved; executive office is made aware of need for and nature of changes in policy, strategic objectives, organizational structures, and allocation of resources.
4. Time required for results	Implemented in stages, with each stage producing significant beneficial results; full implementation may take 4 to 5 years.
5. Character of actual results	Continuous progress toward objectives, much of which should directly affect earnings; short-term results are secured and documented, while further improvement continues to build upon earlier gains.
6. Key roles	Middle and lower management, which develop objectives and improvement plans; upper management, which endorses these and provides resources; chief executive, who actively supports all of these.
7. Key requirement	Maturity—to accept self-control by managers on lower organization levels.

its characteristics are compared in similar terms to the other approaches (see Table 17.2).

The essential difference between this and the other approaches is that it is a continuous process not a one-time project. The primary benefit is a predictable continuity of informational input to the executive office, which forms the basis for informed and intelligent adaptation of policies, objectives, strategies, organizational structures, and facilities to changed conditions. Above all, it provides information feedback on which needed reallocations of the organization's resources can be based.

The management by contract approach is applicable to situations not covered by the other three; it is well adapted to use in an enterprise that is growing and in apparent good health. Morrison and Neuschel noted that executives of seemingly profitable organizations often "have the uneasy awareness that their profits are lessened by millions of dollars from the cumulative drain of many minor inefficiencies, duplications, and marginal activities." To this list can be added the enormous cumulative drain on profit caused by:

- Out-of-date policies, procedures, and practices
- Organizational vacuums and blind spots
- Pockets of inertia
- Blocked communication lines
- Serious underutilization of human resources

BEYOND THE FUNCTIONAL ORGANIZATION

The management by contract process described earlier has been concerned only with the *functional organization* of the firm, that is, the operating organization of people grouped into functions and working together to design, produce, and sell the firm's products and services.

This organizational grouping includes the basic functions of engineering, production (or operations), and sales. It also includes the supporting functions of marketing and all its component activities, such as market research; the many production support activities, such as materials management; and the several sales support functions, such as customer service and order processing. Included, too, are activities that often cross conventional functional department lines, such as capital budgeting, energy conservation, security, and housekeeping.

At this level of the organization, there is a compelling need for structure and process to ensure continuous, systematic upgrading of performance standards in every function and between functions. Without such a discipline, the competitive effectiveness of any enterprise tends to degrade, ultimately to the point where no amount of organizational change or executive exhortation will restore it. The management by contract process is designed to fulfill this need for structure and process.

At this level, too, there is need for firm central direction in order to ensure that the functional organization does not deteriorate into a collection of independent functions performing activities without a common purpose.

This direction must come from outside the functional organization. In the business firm, it is provided by a higher level of organization whose primary function is to guide and control the operating organization so that it continues to fulfill needs in a world in which these needs are constantly changing. This organizational level is represented by the executive office and the board of directors.

The operating organization can be considered as level 1; the directing or executive organization, as level 2. The schematic shown in Figure 17.1 (page 174) depicts the two-level concept.

An analogy may be made with the human organism. Level 1 organization may be likened to the body, with its capabilities to sense its direct environment as well as to perform physical functions. Just as the central intelligence of the organism receives data from its sensors of sight, hearing, touch, etc. and processes it into information that is sent back to the body to guide it in potentially beneficial directions and away from potential harm, so organization level 2 of the enterprise receives data from the "sensors" of the organization (the functions that are in close and constant contact with the external environment—sales, market research, customer service, and others) and processes it into information that serves to control, coordinate, and unify the many disparate individuals and activities on level 1. In carrying out this purpose, organization level 2 *sets objectives* for the functional organization, *formulates strategies* to exploit opportunities and cope with adversities, *allocates resources*, *designs organizational structures* to optimize utilization of the firm's human resources, and *establishes policies* which govern relations with others.

Even as it carries out these functions, level 2 must perform the intellectual task of making informed assumptions about the likely environments in which the organization will operate in the future—a process of creating alternative futures for the enterprise. Failure to perform this demanding task can result in objectives that have a narrow focus and a short time horizon, strategies that can lead the organization into traps and culs-de-sac, organizational structures that misuse or underuse human energies and capabilities, and policies that are out of joint with public perceptions of the firm. Failure can result, as well, in serious misallocation of critical resources in the near term.

The management by contract process has a pronounced beneficial effect on this level of organization by providing it with current data on the firm's external environment as well as with current internal performance standards. This is shown on the schematic as the upward flow of information from the functional level in the form of reports on:

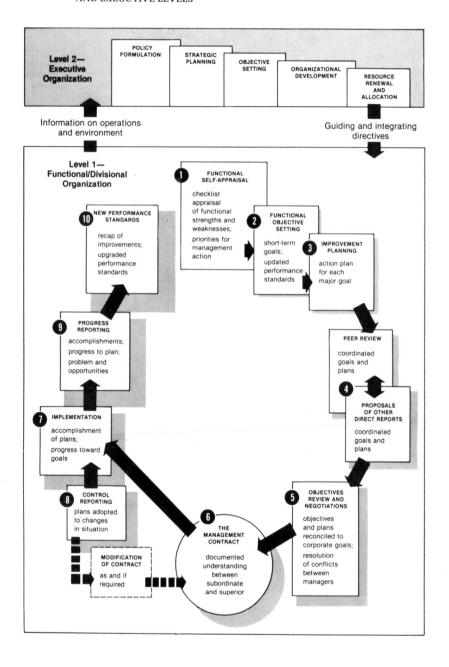

- Periodic results of operations—revenues, costs and expenses, income, cash-flow, variances from budgets
- Performance of people
- Utilization of fixed and working capital resources
- Progress toward objectives
- External changes and developments—markets, competition, legislative and regulatory environment, socioeconomic environment
- Input to strategic and operating planning

The guiding and integrating information that is fed back down to the functional organization takes the form of:

- Policy statements
- Approved objectives for growth and development
- Approved strategic plans
- Organization changes
- Revised delegations of authority
- Approved capital and expense budgets
- Periodic redeployment of resources

The functional organization applies these statements of corporate intent and direction in its everyday business conduct, of course. It utilizes the information as a guide in applying resources, as the basis for setting goals for operational planning, and as constraints on its authority to act for the company. Level 1 also utilizes them as base data for each annual iteration of the management by contract process.

This process of input, activity, and output is similar to that depicted earlier:

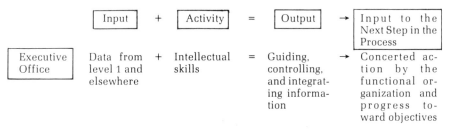

Input	+	Activity	=	Output	→	Input to the Next Step in the Process
Executive Office	Data from level 1 and elsewhere	+ Intellectual skills	= Guiding, controlling, and integrating information	→	Concerted action by the functional organization and progress toward objectives

The functional organization represented by level 1 can continue to operate even if a number of its internal functions are less than fully effective. It can continue even in the total absence of some if market conditions are favorable enough—witness those companies which go on for years lacking a marketing function or new-product planning. The enterprise may suffer, but it can survive for a time. But the functional organization cannot survive for long without the unifying coordination and guidance provided by level 2. When they lack centralized direction, functional people will still continue to act and to react. The operation will not come to a stop, as would a machine cut off from its power source. But it will be only a matter of time until the organization, deprived of its integrating function, will deteriorate into a loose coalition of individual activities, each going its own way uncoordinated with the others—resembling a kind of Brownian motion, incoherent, self-canceling, directionless.

Management by contract provides a mechanism through which the executive level can determine what kind and what degree of direction is needed by the functional organization. It provides a means to identify with greater precision what may be lacking at the lower level in the way of policy guidance, defined objectives, development and growth strategies, identification of future opportunities and jeopardies, and organizational development. The process also provides the executive office with a methodology for allocating resources to the most productive uses.

Most important, the process can provide the executive office with the means to ensure that its policies and strategies are in harmony with the times and the environments in which the enterprise operates.

Despite the facetious notion among lower-level managers that the front office is overpopulated by highly paid and underworked executives enjoying the corporate good life, there is ample evidence that many companies are undermanaged. In this organismic view of the organization that level 2 (the central intelligence of the corporate body) represents, many functions vital to corporate health and survival reside. If these functions are performed inadequately, the effectiveness and productivity of the total organization will be seriously impaired. If these functions are not performed at all the organization will soon cease to exist as a viable entity.

Given proper guidance and strong central direction and provided with motivating overall objectives, an organization of ordinary people can accomplish extraordinary tasks. The efforts and strengths of every individual and function will complement, reinforce, and augment every other and the effect will be genuine synergism within the enterprise.

It almost goes without saying that the operating organization needs the leadership of level 2 people with insight, intellectual capacity, perception, depth and breadth of experience—plus a positive vision of the future that economist/philosopher Kenneth Boulding described as necessary in order to organize the present behavior of the firm.

It was noted earlier that the management by contract process has no upper limit in terms of its applicability. The occupants of the executive office can follow the same procedure as the manager in the field or on the shop floor; each executive can perform the self-appraisal of the position, set objectives, and develop improvement plans. And the executive's productivity will be improved just as readily.

NOTES

¹ Morrison, J. Roger, and Neuschel, Richard F.; Exhibit from "The Second Squeeze on Profits," *Harvard Business Review*, July/August 1962. Copyright by the President and Fellows of Harvard College; all rights reserved. Reprinted by permission of the *Harvard Business Review*.

THE ESSENTIAL PURPOSE
OF ENTERPRISE

The study and research conducted for the writing of this book have led the author to a philosophical proposition with highly practical implications to contemporary management. It can be postulated that there is an even higher level of organization for the enterprise. It becomes necessary, in fact, to do this in order to comprehend how a business organization can endure for generations, as many companies have—even for 3 centuries, as the French glassmaker, Saint Gobain-Pont-à-Mousson, has—surviving through the years a number of changes in ownership and countless management changes. It appears that a strong force for survival is inherent in the business enterprise. Once set in motion, it tends to acquire a somewhat metaphysical existence of its own, one that is unrelated to the specific products and services it produces and the particular markets it serves, independent of the ownership and management in place at any given time, and unperturbed by changes in these factors. If this is so, the enterprise should continue to live on—surviving a succession of owners and managers—conceivably forever.

This higher level of organization—call it the existence level—represents the enterprise as an entity whose purpose is to fulfill economic and social needs. At the risk of stretching our earlier metaphor to the breaking point, this level might be conceived of as the enduring spirit of the enterprise.

At this level, there is a compelling need for a clear and forceful expression of this spirit—a statement of essential purpose and a defining of the primary objectives of the enterprise. This is needed as a constant, unchanging, and inspirational creed or doctrine. It is an article of faith intended to ensure that the policies, subordinate objectives, strategies, and resource allocations of the firm are relevant to the needs and interests of *all* its constituencies, now and in the future, and that they do not become self-

**CHAPTER
EIGHTEEN**

centered upon the small group of owners and managers in place at the moment.

This purpose and these objectives must be larger, broader, and more encompassing than the conventional corporate goals of profit and wealth maximization. This is not an argument for creation of the altruistic organization; to the contrary, profit is a basic need of a business, and maximizing the wealth of the owners is a practical necessity if the firm is to attract the capital necessary for growth and maintenance of its competitive position.

A statement of purpose that has the capability to achieve these goals, while being grander in scope than either, is this: *The essential purpose of the enterprise and the primary objective of its owners and managers is survival and perpetuation of the enterprise.* And it is only through the efficient fulfillment of economic and social needs—the needs of all beneficiaries of the enterprise—that this purpose can be realized.

The need for such an expression of purpose and objectives is very real; it is a practical necessity, not a theoretic assumption. *Without its guidance,* owners and managers will act primarily in their own narrow self-interests and not in those of the total enterprise—that is, not in those of the other constituencies of the enterprise; its employees, its customers, its lenders, its suppliers, its neighbors, its governments, and society in general. *Without its driving force,* lethargy can drain the organization of its energy and vitality and cause the enterprise to lose its competitiveness in the marketplace. *Without its future-orientation,* management will tend to act and decide within a short time horizon, and the future viability of the enterprise will be impaired. *Without its challenge to management,* the business entity is easily subverted from the fulfilling of socioeconomic needs to the serving of the parochial interests of the people in charge at any given time.

The principal cause of business failure can be found here. It can be said with considerable support from business history that businesses do not die of natural causes—they are killed. They are not killed by the outside forces of competition, technological advance, social change, or even by government regulation (onerous as it may appear to be), but from the inside, by their own managements and owners. Competition, technology, and sociocultural change are not hostile forces; they are positive, vitalizing forces acting to strengthen and prolong the life of the enterprise. It is the *internal negative* forces of management inertia, friction, lethargy, narrow purpose, and neglect that cause most of the insolvencies, failures, and bankruptcies.

Figure 18.1   THE MANAGEMENT BY CONTRACT PROCESS VIEWED AS A WHOLE

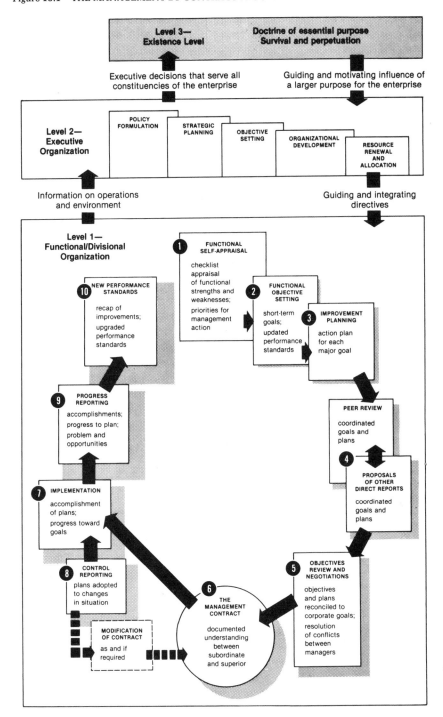

Management by contract, in its broadest conception, recognizes that even as levels 1 and 2 interact and energize one another, level 2 is energized as well by the inspiration drawn from awareness of level 3. Policies, objectives, and strategies can be kept in harmony with the times and current conditions through interaction with level 1; they are prevented from becoming narrow and parochial and focused solely on the "here and now" by the broadening and elevating influence of level 3.

The schematic diagram shown in Figure 18.1 (page 181) illustrates the total management by contract process.

DETAILED PROCEDURE FOR THE FUNCTIONAL SELF-APPRAISAL

*T*his section is intended to provide you with tools to make a self-appraisal of your function. It is in two chapters; the first contains a detailed set of guiding instructions; Chapter 20 contains the complete ten-point Checklist discussed briefly in Chapter 6.

Chapter 6 gave directions for scoring and rating your self-appraisal; it is recommended that you reread these before proceeding with the Checklist appraisal.

It is also recommended that you read Chapter 19, the "Manager's Guide to the Functional Self-Appraisal" before you undertake to respond to the points on the Checklist. It is only fair to warn you that the self-appraisal is tough and demanding. You should allocate sufficient time for the preparation and thought it requires. Some of the points may require access to your files or to those of your subordinates and associates. Aside from this need, it is suggested

PART FIVE

that you conduct your appraisal away from the daily distractions of your workplace.

It was observed earlier that this appraisal covers aspects of functional management that are common to most business functions. It does not get into the technical or professional factors of specific functions themselves; these are well covered by the many handbooks and manuals currently available, such as those published by McGraw-Hill, The American Management Association, and others.*

* The author of this book has prepared a set of self-audit checklists covering some sixty functions of marketing and sales, production operations, and general management. These are in the same format as the general Checklist given here. These are available from the Institute for Business Planning, Inc. (a Prentice-Hall unit), Englewood Cliffs, New Jersey, under the title, "Sixty Ways and Sixty Days to Greater Business Productivity."

MANAGER'S GUIDE TO THE FUNCTIONAL SELF-APPRAISAL

1. GENERAL MANAGEMENT OF THE FUNCTION

A. Business Mission

The important things to know are three, namely

- That your function has a well-defined mission, a statement of purpose or charter, which governs its actions and relationships with others—in other words, that your function operates under a recognized "franchise"
- That the mission is clearly stated in writing and is published in a medium that is available to all persons concerned both within the function and outside it
- That the mission has been reviewed and revised during the past 12 months

A well-defined mission does not by itself make a function effective; lack of it, however, can seriously impair the function's productivity. As a not uncommon example, a marketing department is almost always held accountable for the failure of a new product in the marketplace. But unless the business mission of the function clearly and forcefully spells out the new-product responsibilities of marketing (first, to take the lead in the identification and selection of new-product opportunities and then to assume a major role in their control throughout engineering and development), new products will come from sources unrelated to the marketplace. Intriguing new products inevitably will spring forth from the fertile minds and deft hands of the technical people; once in tangible form, these products tend to take on a life

CHAPTER NINETEEN

and a momentum of their own. Frequently, they can capture the interest of top executives to the point where it becomes impossible to stop the products, despite warning signals from the marketplace.

This is not to say that products that originate in the laboratory always flop in the market; it is simply that, without marketing intelligence, the risk is high that technological successes may become market disappointments.

Your appraisal must first seek assurance that your function has such a mission statement and that it clearly defines the obligations and prescribes the limits of the function. (It is the responsibility of the next higher level of management to ensure that this mission does not duplicate or conflict with that of other functions. This is discussed as a subsequent stage of the process.) Next, assurance must be sought that the mission is documented, that it is not simply in the mind of the manager, and that the document is accessible to all involved, including other functions with which your function interrelates. Obviously, this requires a formalizing of the mission—a transcription from the "back of the envelope" into the business plan, for instance, where it becomes a guiding statement for development of functional objectives and strategies. (A job description of the functional manager is not the business mission of the function, although it may contain information that is relevant.)

Finally, your appraisal must determine whether your mission statement has been reviewed during the past year and amended to reflect the changes in company organization, policies, plans, and strategies that have occurred since it was last formalized. If it has not been revised, the chances are high that it no longer accords with today's realities. If, on the other hand, there have been no significant changes made in the firm's organizational structure, policies, and strategies since your mission was last reviewed, it is likely that the company itself has not kept pace with external change and may be seriously out of phase with its environment.

B. Guidance of
Policies/Objectives/Strategies

The next areas that your appraisal should explore are the ways in which your function is guided by top management policy. It also looks at the extent to which your function's personnel are guided and directed by the company's objectives and strategies. The appraisal must seek to resolve such critical questions as these: are *corporate policies* made known to all persons having a need to know; are they understood; and are the obligations and responsibilities of each to observe these policies made clear and accepted as conditions of employment?

To assume, as many managers do, that the policies of the company are so firm and clear that they need no articulation ("everyone knows *that*"!) is not only risky but unfair. Top management, for example, may consider itself above reproach in the matter of dealings with suppliers and customers, but unless clear and unequivocal statements of policy are issued prohibiting kickbacks and bribes by salespersons and buyers, the executive office must share in the blame when these things happen. The recent history of under-the-table payments to overseas customers by large companies bears this out, and the chief executive officers of several large international corporations have paid a high price for their failure to establish guiding policies in this area.

Policy, by definition, must be firm and evenhanded in applicability, even though a particular policy might be to compromise or to adopt an expedient on occasion. Policy also implies a lasting quality; one can scarcely expect people to follow a policy that vacillates or changes frequently. ("What is our firm and unswerving policy of the day?," asks the company cynic.)

It has been said that a company's policies are a reflection of its relations with others—its attitudes and behavior toward employees, customers, vendors, shareholders, lenders, and the public. To the extent that this is so, policies should be timeless. "Honesty is the best policy" today and will remain the best policy forever. Yet, to say that policies should never change is to run the risk of being inflexible; a policy of assured lifetime employment for all employees can change as government assumes more responsibility for the welfare of people who are without employment.

Moreover, blind acceptance of a policy by employees, without real understanding of its implications to their behavior, carries with it the risk of policy failure. It is not enough simply to issue policy; it must be made absolutely clear to those responsible for its implementation. This implies an obligation on the part of management to educate personnel in policy, to explain policy, and to defend it if need be. There is no risk—a strong policy will stand up, and a weak one will gain strength through this process.

Related to policy, but clearly subordinate to it, are the company's objectives and strategies. These might be viewed as the implementing arm of policy. The appraisal should attempt to determine first whether these vital expressions of company intent are communicated to those who should be aware of them and then to determine the extent to which each individual's required contribution is known and accepted as a personal goal. Objectives and strategies can be sensitive matters, competitive strategies in particular, and not everyone needs to know them.

Expecting responsible managers to perform key roles in carrying out a strategy, however, without informing them about both the strategy and the objective toward which it is directed can only be likened to dispatching a platoon of soldiers into enemy territory without instructions to its leaders. (A tragic example of this was the ill-fated 1980 attempt to rescue the Iranian hostages. A high-ranking military panel appointed to review the operation reported that "several military officers who had critical roles in preparing for the raid were *not fully informed about the aims of the mission.*")

C. Performance Standards

A vitally important element of management, one which transcends the functional structure, is the setting of high standards of performance and measuring achievement of these standards. Your appraisal must seek to know, among other things,

- Whether productivity improvement goals have been set for all definable tasks within your function
- Whether cost reduction targets have been established for each subfunction
- Whether quality standards have been established for all outputs of the function

Further, the appraisal must determine to what extent

- Actual productivity improvements are measured and compared to goals
- The actual amount of money saved through cost reduction is compared to savings budgeted
- The actual quality of output is measured and compared with standards

It is important, also, that your functional people *know* that your standards are high and that their performance is expected to measure up to these standards.

D. Management Training and Development

It has become almost axiomatic in progressive organizations that participation in business planning by all levels of management is essential to good planning. Surprisingly, many apparently successful companies reject this notion as overly democratic and confine involvement in planning to a few selected high-level executives. The appraisal should take a positive position on this issue and evaluate the degree of participation by functional management on the basis of "the more the better."

Your appraisal should take a similar stand on the matter of training and development. There can hardly be too much of it, since few organizations ever do enough of it. Your appraisal should seek, first, to ensure that all personnel, regardless of prior experience, are given training when they join your function and are given periodic retraining as changing conditions warrant. To the extent possible, each person should be trained in other jobs. Personal self-development also is appraised in terms of active encouragement given and opportunity offered.

---

2. STRUCTURE AND ADMINISTRATION OF THE FUNCTION

A. Organization and Staffing

The productivity of human activity of any scale is a fairly direct function of its organizational structure and position. In making an appraisal of your function, the organizational structure must be evaluated in two ways: (1) its internal effectiveness in accomplishing tasks, and (2) the effectiveness with which your function interrelates with other organizational units.

Your appraisal should address both of these areas. It should look first at position in the hierarchy, because the relationship of the function to the total organization can be a more important determinant of its effectiveness than its internal composition. In the business organization, productivity of any function is strongly dependent on its relative position in the total organizational structure, because this is a highly visible indicator of the activity's importance in the eyes of top management. If the marketing department, for example, is several levels down on the charts, the voice of the marketing manager may be muffled by the organizational layers between him or her and the top echelon of the company. As a consequence, engineering, manufacturing, or sales may have a stronger role than marketing in shaping overall policy and strategy; new products may then be selected primarily because they happen to suit the company's existing engineering capabilities, its production facilities, or the preferences of its field sales forces, rather than because they meet the demands of the marketplace. On the current industrial scene, as energy consumption becomes a more significant cost factor, the importance of energy conservation as an activity is being made known to all by the elevation of energy managers to positions on the top executive staff. During the 1980s, emphasis on *productivity* will move productivity managers higher in the organizational hierarchy.

Your appraisal, therefore, should first seek to expose any weaknesses or deficiencies in the way that your function relates organizationally to the other company functions. Is it formally recognized by its position in the structure as an important activity for all to see? Do you report to an authority who is high enough in the hierarchy to make critical decisions on your behalf? Are you privileged by your position to participate routinely in top-level management meetings where major business matters affecting your function are discussed and important action assignments are made? Without such organizational status and visibility, a manager, no matter how personally effective, may have difficulty in persuading the managers of other functions to lend support and cooperation. As a consequence, the function, regardless of how efficiently it may perform its individual activities, will not be productive.

Your appraisal should then review the internal organization of the function to determine whether it is structured in a way that will enhance its effectiveness rather than impair it. It should ask: Are the organization charts current and do they reflect the real organization? Is the organization "lean and clean"? Are internal lines of authority clearly drawn? Do up-to-date position descriptions exist for all key jobs? Are these slots filled with trained, experienced professionals who are well informed about the company, its products, and its markets?

B. Operating Budgets

Assuming that the appraisal has determined that your function is effective in its organizational aspects, the next step is to probe the ways in which its day-to-day activities are administered and operated.

It is almost too obvious for comment that every human activity has a cost implication. Critical to the appraisal of each function, therefore, is assurance that the costs of operating the function have been considered and provided for. This assurance can come only from a formal budget allocation of funds to the function. The appraisal should always be oriented to the future, of course, so the funds provided must be adequate to cover all necessary costs and expenses for the period ahead (normally for the next 3, 6, and 12 months). The assurance that the appraisal seeks can be realized only when the forward estimates of costs and expenses have been developed on an analytical basis of projected needs, not solely upon past experience blended with a mixture of hope and faith. Unfortunately, budgets all too often are based on the latter.

Because this aspect of business operation is so critical and because so much of what follows in our discussion hinges upon sound planning (of which budgeting is a significant part), the next few pages are given to a discussion of the principles involved.

The preparation of operating budgets is an annual tribal rite built into the management routines of most contemporary business firms. Unfortunately, in many sizable and presumably well-managed companies, it is a process that inhibits managerial productivity rather than contributing to its improvement. More often than not it is an exercise in "number crunching," using as its base past experience only—the actual sales, production costs, and departmental expenses of the year just ended or just winding down. The resulting budget is frequently little more than a documentation of last year's actual results percentaged upward or downward by a factor for improvement.

Little regard is given to long-term historical trends or to critical analysis of past events that may have affected actual results. Even less consideration is given to identifying likely external developments that can be expected to affect results during the budget year. As a consequence, operating budgets may be unrelated to the external environment in which the company functions and vulnerable to changes in this environment. Managers attempting to operate by such a budget often find themselves buffeted by events not comprehended in the numbers; they may be forced to divert time from productive tasks to explain or defend variances from budget that are caused by circumstances beyond their control. (In this connection, Drucker has warned against budgets that become more important than the objectives of the firm.)

In many cases, operating managers are not encouraged or even permitted to take an active and constructive part in the development of the budgets. Even in those companies where management considers itself enlightened, middle-level managers' participation is frequently limited to a passive role, in which their individual projections or forecasts undergo a process of topside adjustments to meet predetermined aggregate revenues and net income—a process from which these managers are largely excluded. The effect is that a manager is "given" a budget allocation so at variance with the original submission that the manager neither recognizes it nor feels responsible for it.

This process of adjustment is often an iterative one, which can take considerable time. It is not uncommon for operations to be weeks or months into the budget year before the annual operating budget is approved and released. Any comparison of actual results with budget for the prior elapsed period is then academic and nonconstructive.

In some companies, the budgeting process becomes so elaborate that the procedure creates a staff of professional budget analysts to cope with its complexities. Operating managers become frustrated and convinced, not without justification, that the system has been designed to harass them not help them. They feel victimized by the administrators whose function is to serve them, the producers. Productive effort may then be diverted from beating the budgeted targets to beating the system itself. It's a short step from this to covering failure to meet budgeted levels of revenues or expenses with "creative reporting"—often with the intention to make up for the deficiency in revenues or the overexpenditure in the next reporting period. When this doesn't happen, frequently, like the compulsive gambler on a losing streak, the manager becomes caught in a trap of his or her own devising and may resort to alibis, truth-slantings, and outright lies to cover the shortfall.

John Argenti, in tracing the history of business failures, detected in many a pattern of events in which managers resort to this kind of reporting as the company's position deteriorates.[1] Although itself not the major cause of business failure, "creative" accounting and reporting can greatly lessen real control and accelerate the slide into insolvency of a company that has been weakened by other factors.

Not all organizations demand that department managers detail and justify their current level of expenses before projecting them into the future despite the lessons of experience that teach us that organizations tend over time to take on staff and activities unrelated to their primary purpose and function. Budgeting time is an appropriate time to shed personnel and activities that are unproductive in terms of objectives. This, of course, accounts for the attractiveness of zero-base budgeting, and it can be expected to become a useful management discipline in the future.

One other aspect of budgeting deserves comment. Budget allocations are often used to favor certain functions over others; in this respect, budgets are important signals of company emphasis and intent. At times they can be used to further the ambitions and inclinations of one particularly dominant executive (not always the CEO) to the degree that the budget becomes, in the words of Western

Union vice president Jerry Kent, "The golden rule of business—the guy with the gold makes the rules."

C. Controls and Procedures

Your appraisal should seek to determine next the extent to which current operating and administrative systems, procedures, and standard practices are the product of professional analysis and design and are known and followed by functional personnel. The following questions should be asked: are they effective, are they readily available, and are they reviewed periodically with operating people? If standard procedures don't meet all of these criteria, chances are your function is less than fully productive. It is important to know to what extent day-to-day tasks are guided and governed "by the book," that is, by written systems, procedures, and standard practices, rather than by an intuitive seat-of-the-pants style of operation. Experience tells us that the manner in which a task is performed will change with the passage of time, if only because the individual becomes bored with the job. New employees, often hurriedly trained by existing or departing personnel, will make further changes, until problems develop in downstream operations or transactions. In industrial engineering terms, this phenomenon is known as "creeping methods change," and it is one that must be continually watched and corrected.

Finally, your function must be probed to determine to what extent efforts are being directed toward result-producing tasks and are not being dissipated on nonessential activities that can consume employee time and company money without adding to the company's profitability and competitive capability.

---

3. FUNCTIONAL POWER
AND RESPONSIBILITY

A. Authority

This section of your appraisal gets to the heart of the commitment and support given to your function by the executive office. Every manager, to be effective, must be given authority to manage; without it, there can be little real accomplishment and progress toward objectives. Authority does not simply mean the right to issue commands to subordinates, or to hire and fire people. Position titles, titles of company rank, and other trappings of office are not authority; they are only *indicators* of authority—important ones, to be sure—but they are not to be confused with real authority. In a business organization, real authority flows from formal authorization to expend company funds for materials, equipment, services, and wages; to sign contracts binding on the company; and to utilize company resources. Authority must be real, tangible, visible, and unequivocal. There is no substitute for a formal, written, signed delegation of authority, spelling out the precise scope and defining limits and restrictions to give a manager the authority needed to perform effectively. Conversely, there are few things quite as counterproductive to a manager as authority granted and then withdrawn through denials, withheld resources, budget limitations, restrictions on scope of action, or lack of support from higher management.

B. Responsibility

Responsibility is the assignment that you accept as your "mission" to accomplish. It is what you commit yourself to accomplish with the authority delegated to you, the results you expect to show, the return on the company's investment in you. Phil N. Scheid defined responsibility as a personal characteristic of the individual, as standards of integrity, and as the manner in which the individual and the resources are applied to a task—the attributes imparted to the organization or work assignment.

C. Accountability

Accountability is the third leg of the stool; you have been granted authority to act, you have accepted responsibility for the results of your actions, now you are, accordingly, accountable for failure to achieve these results. Responsibility is the positive aspect of the authority given to you; accountability is the other side of the coin. If you expect to be given credit for carrying out your responsibility, you must accept demerits when results are found wanting. It is just as important to spell out the accountability of a management job as it is to define the job's responsibilities.

Samuel Eilon summed it up in this capsule definition: *authority* is the acknowledged right to command, to make decisions, to take action; *responsibility* is the obligation to act in a given circumstance in a given way; *accountability* is the obligation to explain and justify one's actions.[2]

Lack of authority diminishes the ability to achieve objectives by depriving the manager of the power needed to accomplish tasks.

Failure to define a manager's responsibilities clearly can dissipate and misdirect efforts. Lack of clear accountability may give a manager an escape hatch when things go wrong—something a good manager doesn't need and a weak manager should not be allowed to use.

Of the three, of course, only authority can be delegated. You can grant portions of your assigned authority to your subordinates without loss to yourself; in fact, it is more probable that you will gain from the giving, because you will then be in a position to accept additional authority to replace that which you have delegated. Responsibility and accountability, however, cannot be delegated. No matter how much authority is delegated, you, the granting manager, still retain responsibility and accountability even though your subordinate takes on a share of it as a condition of authority. Your subordinate's responsibility and accountability is to you only, not to those above you.

4. FUNCTIONAL MEASUREMENTS AND CONTROLS

Output, it was stated earlier, is the primary and overriding concern of the functional self-appraisal. Accordingly, the purpose of this section of the appraisal is to focus your attention on the output of your particular function. It seeks first to identify what that output is, as a precondition to evaluating the way in which it is measured, recorded, and controlled.

At this point, you are required to take a giant step beyond convention and define the output of your function in different terms than those you ordinarily use. What, you are asked, is the real measure of the effectiveness of your function? If you are an advertising manager, is the output of your function color brochures, printed advertisements, and TV commercials? Is it measured by the number of ads produced, the number of lines in the print media, the number of commercial seconds on the air? Should its effectiveness be measured by the number of awards received from the advertising associations?

The answer, of course, is that it is none of these. The true output of the advertising function is the number of inquiries received from prospective buyers and the quality of these inquiries in terms of prospects' needs, their ability to buy the product, and their degree of favorable disposition to buy. In the final analysis, therefore, the real output of the advertising function is its *input to the "using" function*—

the sales department—and it is measured by good sales leads produced.

All else is only means to an end. All else is functional input and activity—in a world where only output represents productivity Every measurement, record, and control report used by your function must be concerned with output in these terms, not with reports produced, or surveys made, or studies completed, or products positioned, or meetings held with agencies, or ads produced, or even awards received for advertising excellence.

Output as Driving Input

A powerful force for increased productivity is at work here. The effectiveness of the sales organization, not only in a direct-marketing situation but in many consumer and industrial markets, is critically dependent upon sales leads produced by advertising. Accordingly, in its own interests, the selling function will bring pressure on advertising people to improve the quantity and the quality of advertising response, thereby contributing to enhanced advertising productivity. More and better sales leads in turn increase productivity of the sales force by enabling salespeople to close more sales.

Thus the output of each and every function must be perceived as *the driving input* to the succeeding transaction. Does this hold true for other functions? Yes, it is equally true for every organized activity of the business, whether marketing, sales, engineering, production, or administration. The output of the sales organization, in this concept, is the volume of new business produced through its efforts—its input of new orders to the production function.

It is of little benefit for the firm to have a large dollar backlog of unfilled orders, however, if it does not contain an adequate markup over costs out of which the company covers selling expenses, expenses of managing the company, costs of capital, a provision for future development, profit, and all the other good things the company must provide for in order to survive. The true output of the selling function, then, and the ultimate measure of its effectiveness, is the *gross profit margin content* of the company's order book, its input to the production or product distribution functions.

For a company to regularly book and fulfill orders lacking adequate margin is to impair the financial strength of the enterprise by consuming working capital. Dollar volume booked by the sales function, then, is not a measure of its productivity. Neither is activity; the number of selling hours, sales calls made, sales reports submitted, and demonstrations made are only of concern as they contribute to a higher value of margin content booked per salesperson per day or week or month. That is true sales productivity.

Output of Market Research

The function of market research, to select another function, is an important activity in the contemporary business firm and a vital one if the enterprise is to survive in a highly competitive and rapidly changing world. Many managers of market research pride themselves on the ability of their people to produce reports and surveys which reflect consumer preferences for the company's products, supported by statistics and charts which show, with impressive mathematical precision, how large the market demand is, how fast it is growing, and how large it will be 5 and 10 years hence.

Some recent experiences tend to cast doubt upon the capabilities of market research to provide top management with the assurance it needs to move confidently into new products and new markets. Western Union's costly diversion into direct consumer marketing in the early 1970s—through a subsidiary named "GiftAmerica"—was preceded by some of the most intensive and expensive market research activity since the introduction of the Edsel. The venture was folded quietly after many months of actual operation failed to find a detectable ground swell of demand for gifts that could be ordered by telephone and delivered overnight. The company swallowed a reported loss of some $28 million, and the market research studies that had forecasted success for GiftAmerica were filed away with those earlier ones that had predicted new life for the telegram if only it were given sufficient sales promotion push.

The point of this discussion is not to berate market research for its failures but to caution against mistaking market research activity for output. The product of a market demand analysis function is not compilations of industry and market statistics, reports of consumer interviews, or market growth forecasts. These are reflections of activity only. The output of the function must be viewed as input to other functions—to the functions responsible for the production and distribution of existing products, for the expansion of facilities and capabilities for these products, and for the planning and development of new products and markets.

Viewed from this perspective, the true output of the market research function is a set of firm recommendations on the courses of action which should be taken by all other functions of the business to capitalize on market opportunities. Reports, study results, market surveys, and statistical analysis are nothing more than support for these recommendations. Market research managers who consider their jobs completed when they document and distribute the results of their surveys are not being productive. They are not even doing their jobs. By stopping short of producing a finished product—the recommendations as to how to exploit the market—they are leaving those decisions to others who may be remote from that market.

Output of Other Functions

Moving away from the marketing and sales area, even such operating functions as plant design and layout, methods improvement, plant maintenance, and materials handling are similar in this respect. Each has an input, an activity, and an output phase. Only when the focus of management is on *output* can real gains in productivity be achieved. The real product of plant design and layout is not blueprints but input to production in the form of improved flow of materials, parts, and finished product; the real product of plant maintenance is increased product output through increased up-time of machinery and equipment; and the real output of materials handling is not tons of material moved per day but input to other functions, input of the right materials to the right place at the right time.

In appraising your function, therefore, you must first identify the true output factors that determine the effectiveness of your function, in terms of what input it sends to other functions. Next, you must seek assurance that the records kept by your function are useful in measuring this kind of effectiveness. Then, you must look at the control reports your function creates and at those which it receives from other functions to ascertain whether these are aids to your function's productivity or hindrances to it. The appraisal must question to what extent these records and reports are based on verifiable facts rather than on conjecture and opinion.

Self-control in management, both Drucker and Odiorne contend, is essential to MBO. Self-control is achieved through self-discipline and reliance on one's own resources to make correct decisions. One of these resources is judgment based on experience and intelligence. Even the best judgment, however, can result in a poor decision if a manager lacks adequate guidance in the form of factual historical records, norms, min-max limits, forecasts, schedules, budgets, and plans—standards to which the manager can compare his or her own performance for purposes of evaluation.

A high degree of self-control demands high standards of accuracy, completeness, and currency in control reports and records. Good control reports and records alone cannot make good managers, but they can make good managers a whole lot better. Reports of actual costs versus budgets or standards can automatically flag major deviations for corrective action without the intervention of the department head. Statistical sampling provides control information quickly at low cost. Individual employee performance reports help managers to identify superior performers as well as those in need of training and to isolate problems that may be inhibiting individual or group performance.

Reports Should Be Action-Oriented

Historical records alone, however voluminous, are not adequate; they should be the data base for the reports, which must be action-oriented. Accuracy is a relative term, of course, and two-decimal-point precision is often a needless luxury. Reports that show trends, relationships, and ratios are most effective, especially if they are graphic in form. Charts with upper and lower control limits can trigger corrective action; they are applicable to almost every function with repetitive elements.

Your appraisal should become specific at this point and probe the record keeping and control reporting of your function to determine what records are maintained and used on a regular basis, what factors are covered, and what automatic controls are in place. Then it should question what kind of "early warning indicators" are watched for advance notice of unfavorable developments. Finally, it must explore the reporting on events and developments in those external environments of significance to your function as well as the responsiveness of your function to changes in these environments.

Records kept and reports issued for defensive reasons or out of unquestioned custom are counterproductive. Every piece of paper that enters and leaves your function must have as its purpose the improvement of functional output, the enhancement of real productivity. If it doesn't, you should eliminate it.

---

5. FUNCTIONAL PERFORMANCE ASSESSMENT

The past is not always a reliable indicator of the future, but managers who neglect the lessons of the past do so at their own peril. Those who neglect history, it is said, are destined to repeat it. This section of the appraisal is intended to assist you to examine the past for clues to factors that can affect the future of your function. This section is an extension of and is dependent on the prior one, which appraised the nature, the validity, and the reliability of the control reports and records used by your function; here you should analyze these control reports and records to ascertain what has been happening over the past year or so, as guidance for your future planning.

The performance of any business enterprise as well as that of each function or activity of the business can only be appraised in the light of actual experience. All else is speculation or prophecy. Accordingly, your appraisal should explore at this point the operating history of your function in terms of its actual record of accomplishment in meeting cost and expense budgets, achieving target dates and deadlines for major projects, and improving performance in essential operating areas.

To be valid, your appraisal must be based upon a review of actual records and reports—not upon opinion, which may be biased, or on human memory, which is often fallible.

A good track record during the recent past, while by no means a guarantee, is a favorable indication that future performance of your function can be expected to be good. A record of deteriorating performance, on the other hand, is prima facie evidence that management attention is required, first to arrest the deterioration and then to turn the trend around to a favorable one. Wishing won't make it so—only action will.

Whether past objectives have been met or have been missed is a vital piece of information in setting objectives for the future. So, too, is a record of performance on important tasks—were they accomplished on schedule or were they delayed so that milestone dates were missed? Even more critical is *why* they were missed—was it lack of resources, lack of concentration, lack of effort, or did failure result from the setting of unrealistic schedules and objectives? The *trend* in each of the important performance factors over a period of time is a vital clue to what can be expected in the future. Trends normally do not change abruptly, at least not without severe stresses and strains.

Good management is, if anything, a process of constant improvement. Surpassing your own performance of last month and last year is one of the rewards, as it is in many games and sports. When your records show an improving trend in performance, you can derive some satisfaction and assurance that you have control of the task; a deteriorating trend is a strong warning that control is lacking. You must identify all critical performance indicators regularly—monthly, weekly, even daily in some cases. In many cases, a simple time-series line graph will serve to depict the trend over time. Finally, you should examine history for events that point to fundamental deficiencies and shortcomings in the operation of your function. If there were unfavorable events or developments that impacted performance, you need to search for patterns that will reveal underlying problems and to isolate these from random happenings or Murphy's Law events. Don't waste time solving one-time problems that won't recur anyway.

---

6. FRONT-OFFICE SUPPORT

Every function requires support from the executive office in order to carry out its assigned mission productively as well as to be effective in dealings with other functions. The most tangible and powerful forms of support are, of course, the written delegation of authority to the functional head, approval of the budget allocation, and the relative position of the function on the organization chart. Other forms of top-level support are important, however, and should not be overlooked in making the appraisal of your function and its effectiveness.

The executive office can recognize the importance of a particular activity or function and demonstrate support, guidance, and recognition through the media of policy statements, letters, talks to employees and managers, active participation in progress review meetings, informed comments on progress reports, and in many less visible ways. These expressions of support and their timing can be critically important to your function, particularly during periods of change, when new improvement programs need the fullest cooperation of other departments and functions in order to succeed.

Your appraisal should now seek to determine to what extent this vital kind of support is provided for your function. If it is lacking, it may be that the fault lies not with the executive office for failure to give it but rather with you, the manager of the function, *for failing to demand it* as a necessary condition to your effectiveness.

It is even more important that the executive office provide the kind of support, guidance, and recognition that enhances the productivity of your function. This requires, first of all, that top management accept *output*, not input or activity, as the primary purpose of every function and adopt a philosophy that results are what count, not efforts. Every subsequent act of support for a function must reinforce this policy. Rewards should be given for accomplishment only and should be withheld when it is lacking. This is an argument for adopting an incentive compensation system based on payment of a bonus geared to achievement in place of annual "merit" salary increases that frequently are related more to seniority than to accomplishment and genuine merit.

7. COMMUNICATION AND COORDINATION WITH OTHER FUNCTIONS

John Donne's "No man is an island . . . " was written long before the age of the business manager, but it could well be paraphrased to fit the contemporary business scene. Every manager in a functioning organization is dependent upon every other. It is only through the effective interworking of the whole organizational complex that the enterprise progresses toward its principal objectives. No individual function, however efficient, can do it alone. A poorly functioning department can, on the other hand, act as a drag on the whole organization, particularly if it is a critical link in the chain of transactions; effort can well be spent to correct the conditions causing this drag.

Not infrequently, one particular function is singled out for management emphasis, perhaps reflective of the top executive's preference or business experience—or perhaps the high energy level of an executive concerned with that aspect of operations. On occasion, the efforts to make one function especially efficient can become so intensive that the harmonious interworking of the whole organization is affected. Spencer Tucker has noted that the business organization is an organic whole, not a grouping of separate, performance-maximizing functions. "Very often," he said, "maximizing in one area can cause the whole company's posture to weaken."[3]

Experience tells us that it is seldom that a single function or department in a large organization can be made to perform so well that the company's profit is increased dramatically because of this alone. It is rare that a single program, no matter how brilliantly conceived and implemented, can convert a company's performance from loss to profit. It is not often that a single individual, however talented, can through *his* or *her* actions alone make the difference between success and failure. A program of management by objectives and self-control, however, with emphasis on improving the effectiveness of interaction and interrelationships among functions, coupled with a modest improvement in the internal operating effectiveness of each function, *can* work wonders on the bottom line.

While it is important to bring up to par any functions that are performing at a level clearly below their potential, it may be even more important to direct management attention toward the reduction of frictions and tensions at critical interfunctional junctions within the total system. An analogy can be drawn with a transportation system in which the long-haul portions are efficient but the junctions between these and local facilities are often quite slow and inefficient (as you know, in the time it normally takes to park the car at an airport, check in, and board the aircraft—and repeat the process in reverse at the destination—a modern jet can fly from Chicago to New York.)

Elimination of the interfunctional tensions and conflicts in a human organization requires a major improvement in the organization's communication and information systems. Few business organizations have a free, full, and unrestricted sharing of information among managers at all levels and in all functions. Rarely is there an honest sharing of problems. It is easy and pleasant to share good news; the normal tendency of managers is to keep problems and bad news to themselves—not from intent to conceal, but in the sincere conviction that they can solve the problems without help from "outsiders." Unfortunately, a hidden problem, not unlike a physical ailment kept from the physician, can fester and become either chronic or so serious as to require radical treatment.

Communication is critical to productivity of the organization, if not to the very life of the enterprise. Roy G. Foltz, in *Management by Communications*, states that "The first condition for survival of any organization is for its people to be constantly and accurately informed about its plans and the results of its actions."[4]

MID-APPRAISAL RECAP

Having come this far in your self-appraisal, it might be well to pause and recap what has been accomplished up to this point, with a brief review and summary of the preceding seven appraisal topics.

Assuming that your appraisal has been favorable up to now, that your function has a relatively clean bill of health, it will have provided you with a high degree of assurance

- That your function operates under a clear, written charter that is up to date and known by all concerned—one that clearly defines your scope of operation and specifies your decision limits
- That company policies, objectives, and strategies that affect your function are followed by your people not simply because they are mandated but because they are understood and accepted

- That employees are performing to high standards of output and quality
- That functional personnel have an opportunity to look beyond their immediate tasks toward the future by taking an active part in planning
- That each person is trained for his or her immediate job and at least one job beyond and is stimulated to develop his or her own potential to the fullest

The second group of appraisal points should have assured you

- That your function occupies a place within the company structure that is high enough organizationally and visible enough to give you the clout you need to be fully effective
- That the function itself is well organized and adequately staffed
- That your function will be provided with the money and resources it needs to produce the required results
- That your function is administered and operated more "by the book" than by hunch, guesswork, and intuition—that is, by engineered systems, procedures, and standard practices governing most of its activities (and that these management guides are kept current with changing conditions)
- That all specific tasks important to productivity of your function are assigned and accomplished
- That nonessential activities are minimized

The third group of appraised points was intended to provide you with confidence

- That you have enough authority to get the job done, that responsibilities for results are firmly fixed, and that accountability for failure cannot be dodged
- That the maximum amount of authority is delegated to those subordinates who will take on the responsibility and accept the accountability that authority implies

The fourth section of the appraisal was designed to give you assurance that you are appraising your function's effectiveness in terms of its *output* not its input or activity, that you know what the true output is and how to measure it, and that all records and control reports contribute to functional productivity.

The fifth group of appraisal points should have assured you that, based on hard evidence, past performance has been satisfactory and trends in key measurements are favorable; therefore, major changes should not be needed to correct submarginal conditions.

The sixth group was intended to give you confidence that your function is receiving its share of top executive support, guidance, recognition, and reward as well as assurance that this support is visible enough so that others know and appreciate the importance of your function.

The seventh group covered the critical area of interfunctional relations and coordination of day-to-day activities. It sought to give you assurance that people in your function have active, continuous, and productive contact with people in the other functions that either provide input to your function or are users of its output, in order that your function can avoid becoming self-centered and insular.

Obviously, to the extent that your appraisal to this point has failed to provide such assurances, there is need for corrective action. This is provided for in subsequent steps in the process. First, however, you move on to the appraisal of the capability of your function "to create advantageous change," in the words of Douglas Sherwin.[5]

8. FUNCTIONAL INNOVATION IN METHODS AND TECHNIQUES

First, your appraisal should look at the ways in which present tasks are performed within your function and seek to provide assurance that your subordinates are not content to continue doing things in the same old way but are actively searching for new and better methods and techniques that will improve their output and that of your function.

How the tasks are performed is as important as who performs them. The computer, we all know, holds enormous potential for relieving people of routine day-to-day work and for systematizing complex information-handling tasks such as, for example, scheduling preventive maintenance routines on large numbers of machines or vehicles. It is important to know whether the computer is being used as fully as it might be to store and process data and to display information needed for operations, for control, and for performance measurement. The computer, however, is nothing more than a *tool*, albeit an incredibly complex and efficient one, and should not be regarded as a solution to information problems.

Your appraisal should also seek to determine whether an active effort is made to search out new ideas, new ways of doing the job, innovative techniques of management, new tools, better control systems, new communications media, new materials, and innovative processes for performing your function better and at less cost—that is, to improve productivity. By "active" effort is meant participation in management seminars and training courses such as those offered by the American Management Associations' membership in professional or trade groups, regular reading of current literature, contact with customers and equipment suppliers, and continuing contact with functional counterparts in the industry or profession. It is critically important to know what methods other companies, other industries, and other specialists in your function are using that may be more productive. All of these activities take time and cost money, of course, and they will not be realized without a budget provision for them; good intentions are not enough.

A source of new ideas that is too often overlooked or dismissed is the people around us, particularly those who are actually doing the work or directly supervising it. Solicitation of suggestions from these individuals can lead to valuable improvements in work methods. This must be done with genuine sincerity, or else it may be rejected as "just another suggestion system."

It is dangerously easy for a manager to become insulated from the outside business world and continue doing things the same old way. Change is upsetting and habit is strong. A determined and active effort must be made to force improvement; top management must make it clear through policy statements, budget allocations, *and by example* that every manager is encouraged, even required, to keep up with the state of the art in his or her particular function.

---

9. FUNCTIONAL IMPROVEMENT PROGRAM

It is essential that all personnel within your function actively seek better ways to perform their own tasks, but this is not enough. Assurance must be sought that everything possible is being done to improve and enhance your function's contribution to the total operation. This is the real meaning of the phrase "creating advantageous change."

To accomplish this you might be expected to operate as a member of a team, perhaps the "interfunctional objectives team" suggested by Douglas Sherwin.[6] On occasion, your role will be that of team leader, as manager of the individual function that stands to gain most from improved performance. Objectives of this group are "change objectives," the development of new higher standards not simply the maintenance of established standards.

The question of who sets the objectives is critical in a group effort. Objectives for individual performance—that is, for maintenance functions—can be established either on a top-down or a bottom-up basis; either method is workable depending on the situation. Setting change objectives, on the other hand, requires a free flow and interchange of ideas among a broad group of individuals with a stake in the outcome. No single individual normally has the scope and the authority to set these objectives—often the most important in terms of moving the enterprise forward. It is important that there exist an organized, active, ongoing, interfunctional team effort; that major improvements are managed as projects with clear objectives, tasks, relationships, and shared responsibilities; and that *all* functions involved participate fully. It is important, too, that this effort not deteriorate into "groupthink"; this requires firm leadership and direction.

It must be understood that change objectives are temporary; so, too, is the composition of the team. Once the objectives are accomplished, they become the new performance standards. The team then moves on to new objectives, often with its membership changed.

---

10. FUNCTIONAL RESOURCES

Finally, your appraisal should seek to determine whether you have access to information (increasingly the most important resource) that enables you to estimate your functional workload for the 3, 6, and 12 months ahead. A longer forward time span may infringe on strategic and business planning; the MBO program is not a substitute for long-range planning but is an adjunct and support to it. On the assumption that your appraisal is made in the final quarter of the year, this projection will cover the budget year, the first year of the 5-year plan.

Such information is conveyed in business plans, marketing plans, sales plans, forecasts, budgets, and operating reports. You must have access to appropriate portions of these documents in order to base your functional projections upon hard data rather than upon hunch, conjecture, and "Kentucky windage."

You then have to make a judgment as to the adequacy of the resources at your command to meet the needs of the company for the periods noted. Resources can be in two forms: internal to your function, such as manpower, capabilities, capital and expense budget allocations, equipment, and facilities; and external to your function, such as computer time and capacity, purchased outside services, and support from other functions of the company. Resources that are lacking must be obtained if the functional objectives are to be achieved.

NOTES

[1] Argenti, John, *Corporate Collapse: Causes and Symptoms*, John Wiley & Sons, Inc., New York, 1976.

[2] Eilon, Samuel, *Management Control*, Macmillan & Co., Ltd., London, 1971.

[3] Tucker, Spencer, "A Managerial Control System," *NAA Bulletin*, August 1962.

[4] Foltz, Roy G., *Management by Communications*, Chilton Book Company, Radnor, Pa., 1973.

[5] Sherwin, Douglas, "Management of Objectives," *Harvard Business Review*, May/June 1976.

[6] Sherwin, Douglas, op. cit.

SELF-APPRAISAL CHECKLISTS

(Please refer to Chapter 6 for instructions on how to use, score, and rate these checklists.)

---

1. GENERAL MANAGEMENT OF THE FUNCTION

A. Business Mission

	Yes	No	S/P*
(1) The function operates under a well-defined business mission or statement of purpose that delineates the scope of its activities and guides and governs its relationships with others.	___	___	___
(2) The mission is in writing, not simply in the mind of its manager.	___	___	___
(3) The mission is published in a document that is available to:			
■ Functional personnel	___	___	___
■ Personnel of other functions having a need to know	___	___	___

CHAPTER TWENTY

* Sometimes or Partially

	Yes	No	S/P*

(4) The mission has been reviewed *and revised* during the past 12 months. ___ ___ ___

B. Guidance of Policies/Objectives/Strategies

(1) Corporate policies are made available to all functional personnel having a need for such guidance. ___ ___ ___

(2) Policies are known and understood by those whose actions they govern. ___ ___ ___

(3) Functional personnel have been informed through meetings and individual discussions about their obligations and responsibilities to these policies. ___ ___ ___

(4) Changes in policy are communicated promptly to appropriate personnel and are explained. ___ ___ ___

(5) Recommendations for policy changes are sent up for executive consideration. ___ ___ ___

(6) Corporate objectives are communicated to functional personnel to the extent appropriate for effective job performance. ___ ___ ___

(7) Corporate strategies and plans are communicated to functional personnel to the extent consistent with company security. ___ ___ ___

(8) Functional objectives are known to all personnel. ___ ___ ___

(9) Each person's required contribution to these goals is known and accepted as a personal goal. ___ ___ ___

(10) All such personnel have been advised that strategies are "company confidential" information. ___ ___ ___

C. Performance Standards

(1) Standards have been set for the performance of all major functional tasks. ___ ___ ___

(2) These performance standards are documented in job descriptions and are available to effected personnel. ___ ___ ___

(3) All functional people know that their performance is being measured and compared to high standards. ___ ___ ___

* Sometimes or Partially

	Yes	No	S/P*

(4) Standards are reviewed regularly and revised periodically. ___ ___ ___

(5) Actual performance is recorded and compared to standards frequently. ___ ___ ___

(6) Productivity improvement goals have been set for all definable tasks. ___ ___ ___

(7) Actual productivity improvement is compared with goals at least quarterly. ___ ___ ___

(8) Cost reduction targets in dollars and percents have been established for each subfunction. ___ ___ ___

(9) Actual cost savings are compared to target amounts and percentages at least every quarter. ___ ___ ___

(10) Quality standards have been set for all outputs of the function. ___ ___ ___

(11) The actual quality of output is measured and compared with standards quarterly. ___ ___ ___

(12) Deficient performance, excess costs of output, substandard productivity, and unacceptable quality are analyzed and corrected through retraining, job redesign, or reassignment of personnel. ___ ___ ___

D. Management Training and Development

(1) All functional personnel take part in planning in a meaningful and productive way. ___ ___ ___

(2) All personnel are encouraged to participate in MBO in an active and purposeful manner. ___ ___ ___

(3) All personnel are given training when they join the function, regardless of prior experience. ___ ___ ___

(4) The functional manager takes an active part in this training. ___ ___ ___

(5) All personnel are given periodic retraining. ___ ___ ___

(6) Each person is given the opportunity to be trained for at least one other job. ___ ___ ___

(7) All employees are encouraged to take advantage of opportunities for self-development, both inside and outside the company, and to prepare for higher responsibility through their own efforts. ___ ___ ___

* Sometimes or Partially

Yes   No   S/P*

(8) Self-control by managers is encouraged and practiced to the maximum extent consistent with company policy.

TOTAL POINTS ☐ +0+ ☐ = ☐

RATING:

$$\frac{\text{Enter number of points scored}}{\text{Enter number of items on checklist}} \boxed{} = \boxed{} \times 100 = \boxed{ \%}$$

2. STRUCTURE AND ADMINISTRATION OF THE FUNCTION

A. Organization and Staffing

Yes   No   S/P*

(1) The function is recognized in published policy statements as an important company activity. ___ ___ ___

(2) The function occupies a position on a high enough level of the organization hierarchy to be visible to top management and effective in its relations with other functions. ___ ___ ___

(3) The function's position in the organization reflects accurately the importance of the function to the enterprise. ___ ___ ___

(4) The function is shown in its proper position on current organization charts. ___ ___ ___

(5) The manager of the function reports to an authority high enough in the organization to make critical decisions on behalf of the function. ___ ___ ___

(6) The manager of the function takes part routinely in top-level meetings where major business matters affecting the function are discussed and important actions are assigned. ___ ___ ___

(7) The organizational relationship of the function to other functions is known and understood within the function and by others. ___ ___ ___

(8) Working relationships with the other functions of the business have been reviewed and updated within the past 12 months. ___ ___ ___

(9) The internal organization of the function is designed to carry out its business mission effectively. ___ ___ ___

(10) The functional organization charts are current, and they reflect the "real" organization. ___ ___ ___

* Sometimes or Partially

Yes No S/P*

(11) Lines of authority within the function are clearly drawn. — — —

(12) The organization is structured in accordance with modern organization principles. — — —

(13) All key positions on the organization charts and the table of organization are filled. — — —

(14) Key positions are staffed by professional managers, trained and experienced in their functions. — — —

(15) Key managers are well informed about the company, its products and services, and its markets. — — —

(16) Even if the function is not a full-time activity, personnel assigned to it are trained and experienced. — — —

B. Operating Budget

(1) The function has a formal budget covering all major aspects of its operation: income, costs, and expenses. — — —

(2) The budget is broken down into functional responsibilities. — — —

(3) The budget was developed through an intensive analytical review of all the function's tasks and responsibilities. — — —

(4) All key functional managers provided input to the proposed budget. — — —

(5) Consideration was given to reduction of expenses, elimination of tasks, and reassignment of personnel no longer essential to functional productivity. — — —

(6) The budget is broken down by months for continuous control. — — —

(7) All costs and expenses are covered, including costs of outside purchased services if required. — — —

(8) The budget was based on a *projection of needs* for the 3, 6, and 12 months ahead (not simply on a percentage change from the prior year). — — —

C. Personnel Controls

(1) The department has a formal, written, internal delegation of authority. — — —

* Sometimes or Partially

Yes No S/P*

(2) Delegation of authority has been reviewed and updated within the past 12 months.   ——— ——— ———

(3) Job or position descriptions are in writing and up to date for all key positions.   ——— ——— ———

(4) Job descriptions contain specific performance standards for all major elements of work.   ——— ——— ———

(5) Job descriptions are revelant to actual work assigned and performed.   ——— ——— ———

(6) Procedures and standard practices are readily available to all personnel.   ——— ——— ———

(7) Procedures and standard practices are in writing and up to date.   ——— ——— ———

D. Internal Communications

(1) Functional staff meetings are held regularly—at least monthly.   ——— ——— ———

(2) All key managers attend and actively participate.   ——— ——— ———

(3) The meetings are conducted according to an agenda published in advance.   ——— ——— ———

(4) Action assignments are recorded and published.   ——— ——— ———

(5) Action assignments are followed up until completed.   ——— ——— ———

(6) Lower level personnel are invited to attend, on a rotating basis.   ——— ——— ———

(7) A general meeting of all management personnel is held periodically—at least every quarter.   ——— ——— ———

(8) Management people are brought up to date on new developments of significance to them and their company.   ——— ——— ———

(9) Each attendee is expected to make a brief presentation on his or her progress on plans and goals.   ——— ——— ———

(10) The activities of all functional personnel are reviewed periodically to ensure that they are directed to useful end results.   ——— ——— ———

TOTAL POINTS   □ +0+ □ = □

RATING:

$$\frac{\text{Enter number of points scored}\quad \square}{\text{Enter number of items on checklist}\quad \square} = \square \quad \times 100 = \boxed{\%}$$

* Sometimes or Partially

3. FUNCTIONAL POWER AND RESPONSIBILITY

Yes　No　S/P*

A. Authority

(1) Authority has been delegated to the function (through formal delegation to the department head) to expend company funds, sign contracts, and utilize company resources for the express purpose of carrying out the assigned mission of the function.　　—— —— ——

(2) The delegation of authority is in writing.　　—— —— ——

(3) The delegation of authority contains dollar limits on spending authority for particular purposes, above which the expenditure requires approval of a specified higher authority.　　—— —— ——

(4) The spending authority of the function is confirmed by allocation of funds to the function through the budget mechanism.　　—— —— ——

(5) The authority of the function to utilize company resources is certified by the published mission statement and published position descriptions of key managers.　　—— —— ——

(6) Authority has been redelegated within the function to subordinates to the maximum permitted by company policy.　　—— —— ——

(7) During an extended absence of the department head, all authority is redelegated to one or more subordinates.　　—— —— ——

B. Responsibility

(1) The head of the department or function has been assigned firm responsibility, through a policy statement or position description, to staff and manage an organization capable of performing the department's stated mission effectively and economically.　　—— —— ——

(2) Responsibility is assigned to the department head to coordinate and control the activities of the function, internally and with other company functions.　　—— —— ——

(3) Key functional managers are responsible for the productive utilization of all resources, including human resources, assigned to them.　　—— —— ——

(4) Responsibility is firmly assigned to the department head to implement enlightened per-

* Sometimes or Partially

Yes No S/P*

sonnel policies within the function, such as to ensure, within budget constraints, the fullest possible personal and professional development of all people reporting to him or her. ___ ___ ___

(5) Responsibility for individual performance and results is vested in each individual (self-control). ___ ___ ___

C. Accountability

(1) The head of the department or function is held accountable for failure of the function to meet its performance standards. ___ ___ ___

(2) The department head is held accountable for failure of the function to meet its department objectives or to meet its obligations to other company functions because of substandard performance by individuals or groups within the department. ___ ___ ___

(3) The department head is held accountable for failure to meet the department's equal employment opportunity affirmative action plan objectives. ___ ___ ___

(4) The department head is held accountable for excess costs and expenses over amounts specified in the operating budget. ___ ___ ___

(5) The department head is held accountable for serious failure to accomplish projects and programs on time and within cost (including projects led by the department that involve other departments) when this is a result of inadequate coordination and control. ___ ___ ___

(6) Key functional managers are held accountable for failure of resources assigned to them to generate an economic return, for loss or destruction of resources, and for serious and repeated failure to meet personal goals. ___ ___ ___

(7) Individual members of the function are held accountable for the consequences of serious breaches of policy and for serious and repeated failure to perform assigned tasks. ___ ___ ___

TOTAL POINTS [ ] +0+ [ ] = [ ]

RATING:

$$\frac{\text{Enter number of points scored} \quad [\quad]}{\text{Enter number of items on checklist} \quad [\quad]} = [\quad] \times 100 = [\quad] \%$$

* Sometimes or Partially

4. FUNCTIONAL MEASUREMENTS AND CONTROLS

	Yes	No	S/P*
(1) Performance standards have been established for all major elements of functional output.	—	—	—
(2) Records are kept of the *output* of the function, in total, by sections, if appropriate, and by individual producers.	—	—	—
(3) The amount of output is routinely and regularly compared with:			
■ A comparable prior period	—	—	—
■ Current performance standards	—	—	—
■ Improvement goals	—	—	—
(4) This comparison is made every month and quarter, at a minimum.	—	—	—
(5) When output in a period falls below standard, it triggers an automatic response (such as temporary staffing or overtime).	—	—	—
(6) When output remains below standard for a predetermined number of periods, it triggers a second-level response (such as notification of department head).	—	—	—
(7) Quality standards have been established for all major output elements.	—	—	—
(8) The quality of output is routinely and regularly measured, recorded, and compared with standards.	—	—	—
(9) When quality of output falls below standards, it triggers an automatic response (such as stopping production until the cause is identified and corrected).	—	—	—
(10) Statistical sampling methods are used to measure quality of high-volume output.	—	—	—
(11) Productivity standards have been set for all major output factors.	—	—	—
(12) Productivity of the function is routinely recorded and measured by acceptable output per hour, per day, or per week, as appropriate—in total, by sections, and by individual producers.	—	—	—
(13) Productivity improvement targets have been established for all major tasks.	—	—	—

* Sometimes or Partially

Yes No S/P*

(14) When productivity of the function falls below standard, it triggers an automatic response (such as analysis of output records to determine causes).   ____ ____ ____

(15) Productivity records are routinely reviewed to identify areas of high and low productivity.   ____ ____ ____

(16) A predetermined set of corrective actions for problem situations takes place automatically, without the active intervention of the manager (such as requiring a revised "cost-to-complete" estimate when an outside contractor overruns costs-to-date by an established percentage).   ____ ____ ____

(17) Project controls are maintained showing actual performance against plan and expenditures versus budget.   ____ ____ ____

(18) Control reports show current status of major programs, actual performance toward objectives and strategies, and status of new development projects.   ____ ____ ____

(19) Major deviations from plans and standards are flagged automatically for management attention.   ____ ____ ____

(20) Reports on overall company performance, such as sales, gross margins, new orders, selling expenses, order backlogs, cancellations, and lost business are routinely received and analyzed for significance to functional activities.   ____ ____ ____

(21) Wherever appropriate, reports, market surveys, and special studies on products and markets are abstracted, cross-indexed, and filed for quick and frequent reference.   ____ ____ ____

(22) Functional progress-review meetings are held at least quarterly to review major projects and programs.   ____ ____ ____

(23) These meetings:
- Are held on a fixed schedule   ____ ____ ____
- Work to a prepared agenda, issued in advance   ____ ____ ____
- Include participation by all other functions involved   ____ ____ ____
- Issue and follow up action assignments   ____ ____ ____

(24) Serious program schedule slippage and cost overruns are assigned to responsible individuals for corrective action.   ____ ____ ____

* Sometimes or Partially

	Yes	No	S/P*

(25) Weekly and monthly progress reports are prepared by all management personnel. — — —

(26) Key reports received from other functions are logged in, and late reporters are followed up routinely. — — —

(27) Key reports issued by the function are logged out and reviewed regularly for compliance with scheduled release dates. — — —

(28) Serious lateness or repeated lateness is corrected through changes in procedure or reassignment of responsibility. — — —

(29) All reports received and issued are reviewed periodically for accuracy, completeness, and compliance with standard practice. — — —

(30) An annual review is made of all reports and records used or issued in terms of their value and need relative to their cost. — — —

(31) Reports and records that have outlived their usefulness or whose cost is disproportionate to their value are discontinued. — — —

(32) A chronological record is kept of internal and external events and developments that have an impact on functional performance or that may affect future plans. — — —

(33) This record is reviewed during the annual assessment of performance (covered in the next section of the self-appraisal). — — —

(34) Postcompletion audits are made of all major projects and program plans to compare actual results with the projections made earlier. — — —

(35) A set of "distant early warning" reports is used to alert functional management to potential threats and opportunities in time to take effective action. — — —

(36) All major activities of functional personnel are guided and governed by written procedures and standard practices. — — —

(37) Functional procedures and standard practices have been developed and written by systems professionals, based on intensive study of the operation and the relationship of its work to other functions. — — —

(38) Changes in procedures are reviewed with affected personnel *before* they are put into effect (preferably in the design stage). — — —

* Sometimes or Partially

Yes No S/P*

(39) Recommendations for changes in procedures to improve productivity made by functional personnel are welcomed and are given serious consideration.   ___ ___ ___

(40) Procedures and standard practices are audited periodically by systems professionals and are updated to reflect new conditions and standards.   ___ ___ ___

(41) Noncompliance with procedures and standard practices is corrected through retraining, job redesign, or reassignment of personnel.   ___ ___ ___

(42) The effectiveness of personnel development is determined by the department's ability to:

- Attract, retain, and promote superior people   ___ ___ ___
- Motivate employees to self-development   ___ ___ ___
- Accomplish challenging objectives   ___ ___ ___

(43) Records are routinely kept of employee progress, accomplishments, and participation in self-development activities.   ___ ___ ___

(44) Organization charts, position descriptions, and assignment tables are kept current.   ___ ___ ___

(45) Internal records and reports are prepared and maintained on a routine basis for the purpose of:

- Keeping the organization staffed with competent people   ___ ___ ___
- Assuring that all personnel know and understand their roles and responsibilities   ___ ___ ___
- Keeping tasks and assignments on cost and time schedules   ___ ___ ___
- Keeping departmental expenditures within budget   ___ ___ ___
- Directing and controlling outside purchased services   ___ ___ ___
- Ensuring that all meetings have a productive purpose and result (agenda and action assignments)   ___ ___ ___
- Ensuring that good information is made available for top-level meetings   ___ ___ ___

(46) Control reports give early warning to management about organizational problems and deficiencies that could adversely affect company profitability or functional productivity.   ___ ___ ___

* Sometimes or Partially

Yes　No　S/P*

(47) Actual expenses are routinely compared with budget every month, and variances are analyzed for corrective action. ___ ___ ___

(48) In periods of high unfavorable variances, expenses are tracked on a shorter time cycle, such as weekly. ___ ___ ___

(49) Individual expense vouchers are reviewed regularly for compliance with expense allowances, and repeated offenders are disciplined. ___ ___ ___

TOTAL POINTS ☐ +0+ ☐ ☐

RATING:

$$\frac{\text{Enter number of points scored} \quad \boxed{}}{\text{Enter number of items on checklist} \quad \boxed{}} = \boxed{} \times 100 = \boxed{} \%$$

5. FUNCTIONAL PERFORMANCE ASSESSMENT

(1) A thorough and objective review has been made of past performance as reflected in control reports and records for the past year. ___ ___ ___

(2) On the basis of this review, the operating performance of the function shows an improving track record in all critical areas. ___ ___ ___

(3) During the past year, there were fewer out-of-control situations that required the intervention of next higher management level. ___ ___ ___

(4) During the past year, the function has met or exceeded overall department objectives. ___ ___ ___

(5) All individual projects were completed essentially within original cost and time schedule. ___ ___ ___

(6) All individual managers have essentially met their personal goals, with few cases of intervention by the manager. ___ ___ ___

(7) All major companywide programs led by the function have essentially met target goals. ___ ___ ___

(8) During the past year, there has been an improving trend in:

- Timing and quality of functional reports ___ ___ ___
- Actual performance versus functional plans ___ ___ ___
- Productivity of functional personnel ___ ___ ___
- Expenses versus budget ___ ___ ___

(9) All functional surveys and studies made during the past year were comprehensive and credible and were completed on time and within cost estimates. ___ ___ ___

* Sometimes or Partially

Yes No S/P*

(10) The function has met its operating budget for the past year, within acceptable tolerances. ___ ___ ___

(11) During the past year:

- At least one open management position was filled by promotion from within ___ ___ ___
- At least one open position was filled by internal transfer ___ ___ ___
- At least one open position was filled from outside ___ ___ ___

(12) During the past year, the only losses of exceptional people were through promotion. ___ ___ ___

(13) During the past year, no major position was left unfilled for longer than 3 months. ___ ___ ___

(14) During the past year, at least one management position was filled by a woman or a minority person. ___ ___ ___

(15) At least 25 percent of department personnel are actively pursuing educational advancement.

TOTAL POINTS ☐ +0+ ☐ = ☐

RATING:

$$\frac{\text{Enter number of points scored} \quad \boxed{}}{\text{Enter number of items on checklist} \quad \boxed{}} = \boxed{} \times 100 = \boxed{} \%$$

---

6. FRONT-OFFICE SUPPORT

(1) The executive office demonstrates active and visible support to the function through:

- Wrtten delegation of authority ___ ___ ___
- Approval of operating and capital budgets ___ ___ ___
- Policy statements endorsing functional projects and programs ___ ___ ___
- Periodic visits to field offices or other facilities ___ ___ ___

(2) Active guidance to the function is provided by top management by means of:

- Frequent direct communication with the head of the function ___ ___ ___
- Informed comments on progress reports and draft proposals ___ ___ ___

* Sometimes or Partially

Yes   No   S/P*

- Active participation in new-plans presentations and progress reviews   —— —— ——

(3) Top management demonstrates confidence in functional management through:

- Appointment of the function head to high-level committees and task groups   —— —— ——
- Approval of funds for management development   —— —— ——
- Recognition and reward for outstanding accomplishments

TOTAL POINTS   ☐ +0+ ☐ = ☐

RATING:

$$\frac{\text{Enter number of points scored} \quad \boxed{}}{\text{Enter number of items on checklist} \quad \boxed{}} = \boxed{} \times 100 = \boxed{} \%$$

7. COMMUNICATION AND COORDINATION WITH OTHER FUNCTIONS

—— —— ——

(1) A minimum of 20 percent of the time of the head of the function is spent on coordinating activities with other functions.   —— —— ——

(2) Cooperation with others is fostered by examples of mutual trust and good faith.   —— —— ——

(3) Communication with other functions is achieved through personal contact and:

- Exchange of MBO goals   —— —— ——
- Exchange of plans   —— —— ——
- Exchange of progress reports   —— —— ——
- Reciprocal attendance privileges at department meetings   —— —— ——
- Participation in task group assignments   —— —— ——

(4) Close working relations and active personal contact is maintained with other functions at several organization levels.   —— —— ——

(5) Functional personnel are encouraged to participate in crossfunctional task force assignments.   —— —— ——

(6) All information that can be useful to others in their day-to-day operations is conveyed to them promptly.   —— —— ——

* Sometimes or Partially

Yes No S/P*

(7) Problems that potentially may involve two functions or that may concern the interrelationships between two functions are reported promptly to the manager responsible for both functions (even while efforts to resolve them may be made at the functional level).

TOTAL POINTS ☐ +0+ ☐ = ☐

RATING:

$$\frac{\text{Enter number of points scored}}{\text{Enter number of items on checklist}} \boxed{} = \boxed{} \times 100 = \boxed{} \%$$

---

8. FUNCTIONAL INNOVATION

(1) Functional managers actively keep themselves informed about new and improved methods, materials, tools, processes, controls, and procedures to perform tasks with less effort and less cost.

(2) Functional managers actively keep up with the state of the art of their function through:

- Seminars, workshops, and conferences
- Professional associations
- Industry contacts
- Review of current literature
- Outside specialists
- Trade associations and publications
- Solicitation of ideas and suggestions from personnel at all levels

(3) Functional expense budgets provide funding for these purposes.

(4) The computer is used to store, process, and display information needed by functional personnel.

(5) The computer is used for control of major plan variables whenever it is determined to be cost-effective.

(6) Cost-effective and timely communications methods are employed for transmission and receipt of information to and from others, including, as appropriate:

* Sometimes or Partially

	Yes	No	S/P*

- Dataphone
- Telex/TWX
- Facsimile
- Audio/video cassettes
(7) Latest techniques of management science in modeling, statistical analysis, and other OR techniques are investigated and adopted when appropriate and cost-effective.
(8) Innovation and creative thinking on the part of all people are encouraged and stimulated by a formal system of top-level recognition and incentive reward.

TOTAL POINTS ☐ +0+ ☐ = ☐

RATING:

$$\frac{\text{Enter number of points scored} \quad \boxed{}}{\text{Enter number of items on checklist} \quad \boxed{}} = \boxed{} \times 100 = \boxed{} \%$$

---

9. FUNCTIONAL IMPROVEMENT PROGRAM

(1) There is an active ongoing program to improve functional efficiency, functional productivity, and coordination and control of the function.

(2) Major effort is directed toward:

- Broader participation in MBO and planning
- More meaningful performance reviews
- Increased participation in management development
- More automatic "self-controls"
- Increased exposure of functional personnel to top management and vice versa
- Improved marketing orientation of personnel and customer responsiveness
- Better progress reporting
- Improved coordination with other functions
- Productive innovation and creativity by personnel throughout the organization.

TOTAL POINTS ☐ +0+ ☐ = ☐

RATING:

$$\frac{\text{Enter number of points scored} \quad \boxed{}}{\text{Enter number of items on checklist} \quad \boxed{}} = \boxed{} \times 100 = \boxed{} \%$$

* Sometimes or Partially

10. FUNCTIONAL RESOURCES

Yes   No   S/P*

(1) Functional managers are kept informed about the company's major objectives, policies, plans, and programs through:

- Participation in key meetings   ___ ___ ___
- Access to appropriate sections of business plans, capital budgets, business development plans, and new product/market plans   ___ ___ ___

(2) Functional managers are kept up to date on important new developments through progress reviews, meetings, and access to key operating reports.   ___ ___ ___

(3) On the basis of this knowledge, the department's workload is known for the next 3, 6, and 12 months.   ___ ___ ___

(4) On the basis of this knowledge and the preceding evaluation, functional resources are judged to be adequate to meet the needs of the company during the next 3, 6, and 12 months, in terms of:

- Manpower   ___ ___ ___
- Internal capabilities   ___ ___ ___
- Facilities and equipment   ___ ___ ___
- Expense budget funding, including outside contract services   ___ ___ ___
- New capital expenditures funding   ___ ___ ___
- Information systems support   ___ ___ ___
- Training support   ___ ___ ___
- Computer time and capacity   ___ ___ ___
- Communications capability and support   ___ ___ ___
- Support from other company functions   ___ ___ ___
- Access to outside resources   ___ ___ ___
- Top-level support   ___ ___ ___

TOTAL POINTS ☐ +0+ ☐ = ☐

RATING:

$$\frac{\text{Enter number of points scored} \quad \boxed{}}{\text{Enter number of items on checklist} \quad \boxed{}} = \boxed{} \times 100 = \boxed{} \%$$

* Sometimes or Partially

INDEX